Welcome to Your Monster Truck Adventure!

Get ready to rev up your engines and unleash your creativity with our exciting monster trucks! Each page brings a new truck to life, from towering tires to mighty engines. Remember, there's no right or wrong way to color these pages—just follow your imagination!

Tips for Coloring Fun:

- Experiment with Colors: Try different combinations and see how vibrant your trucks can become.
- Stay Inside the Lines: Try your best to keep your coloring neat, but if you go outside the lines, no worries—it's all part of the fun!
- Share Your Art: Show your finished pages to family and friends. Maybe they'll join in too!

Now, turn the page and start your engines. Your first monster truck is waiting for you!

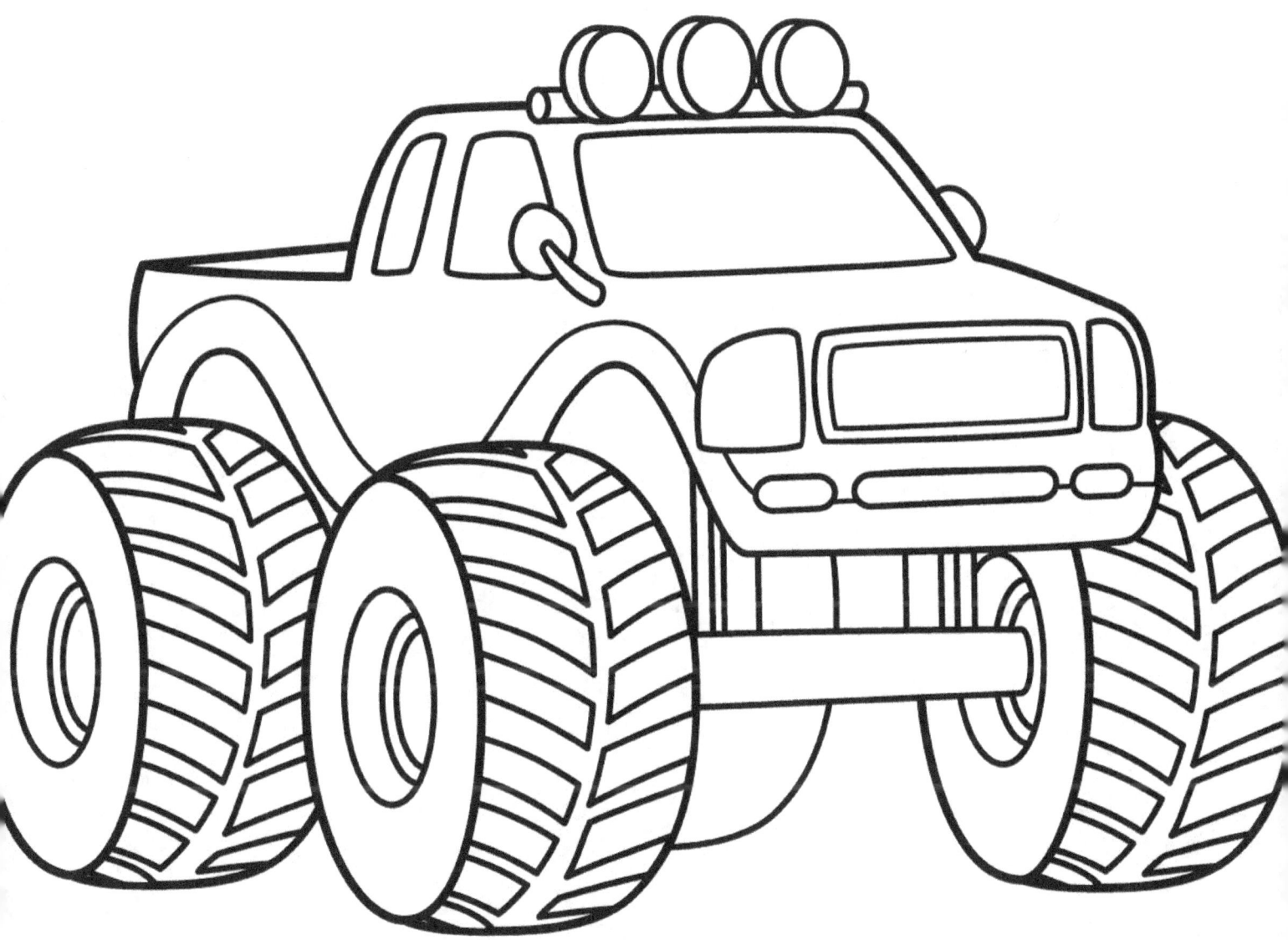

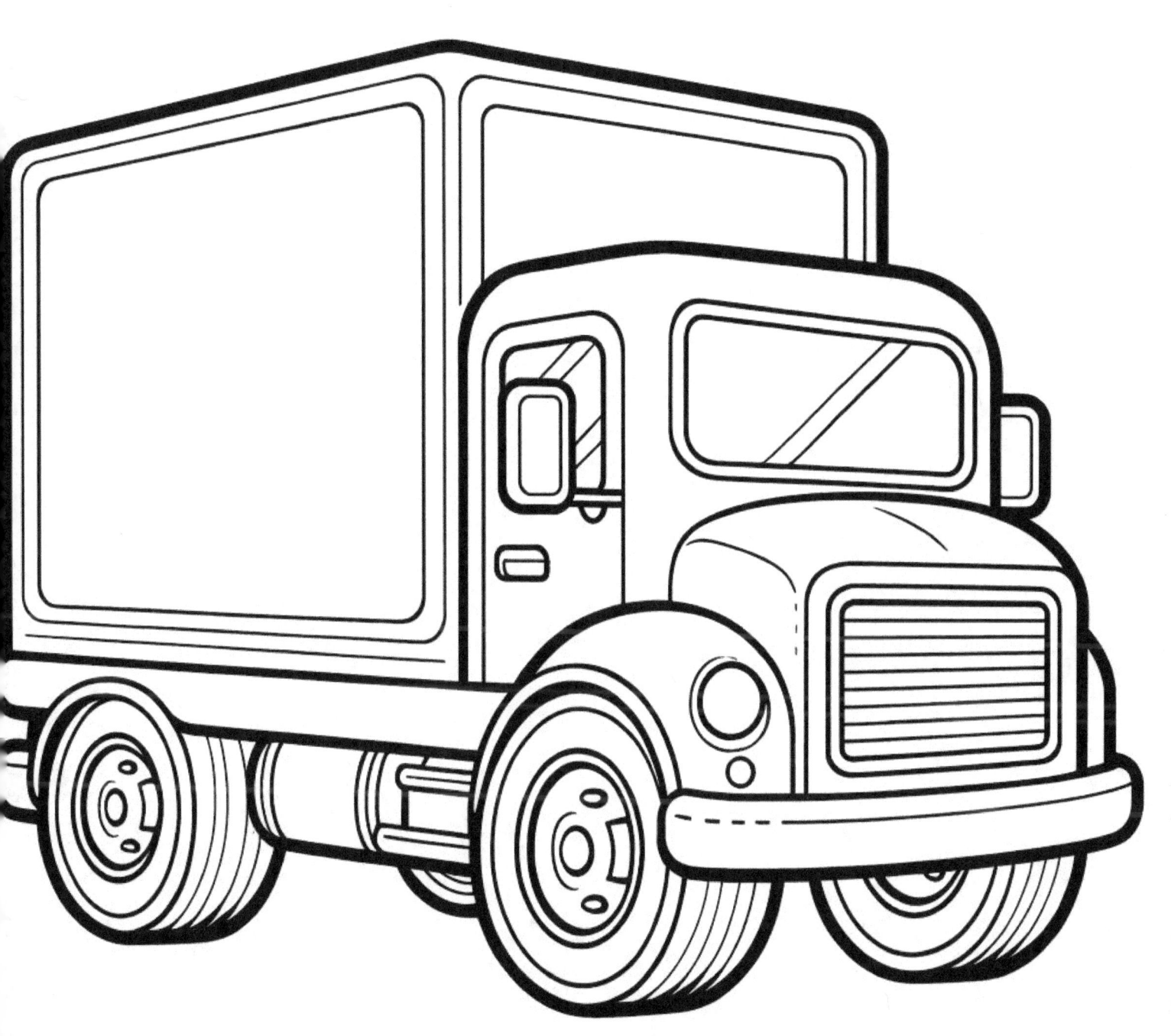

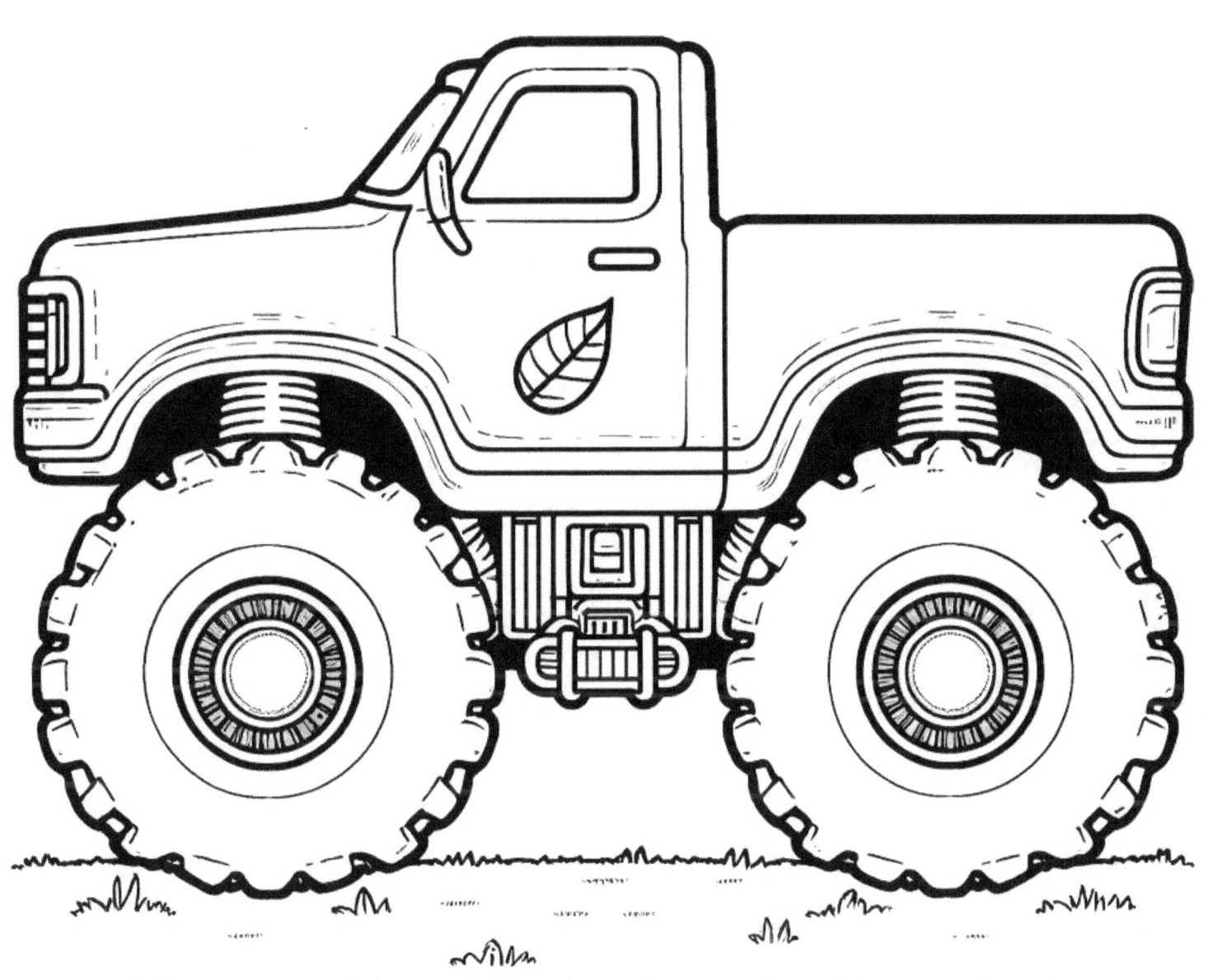

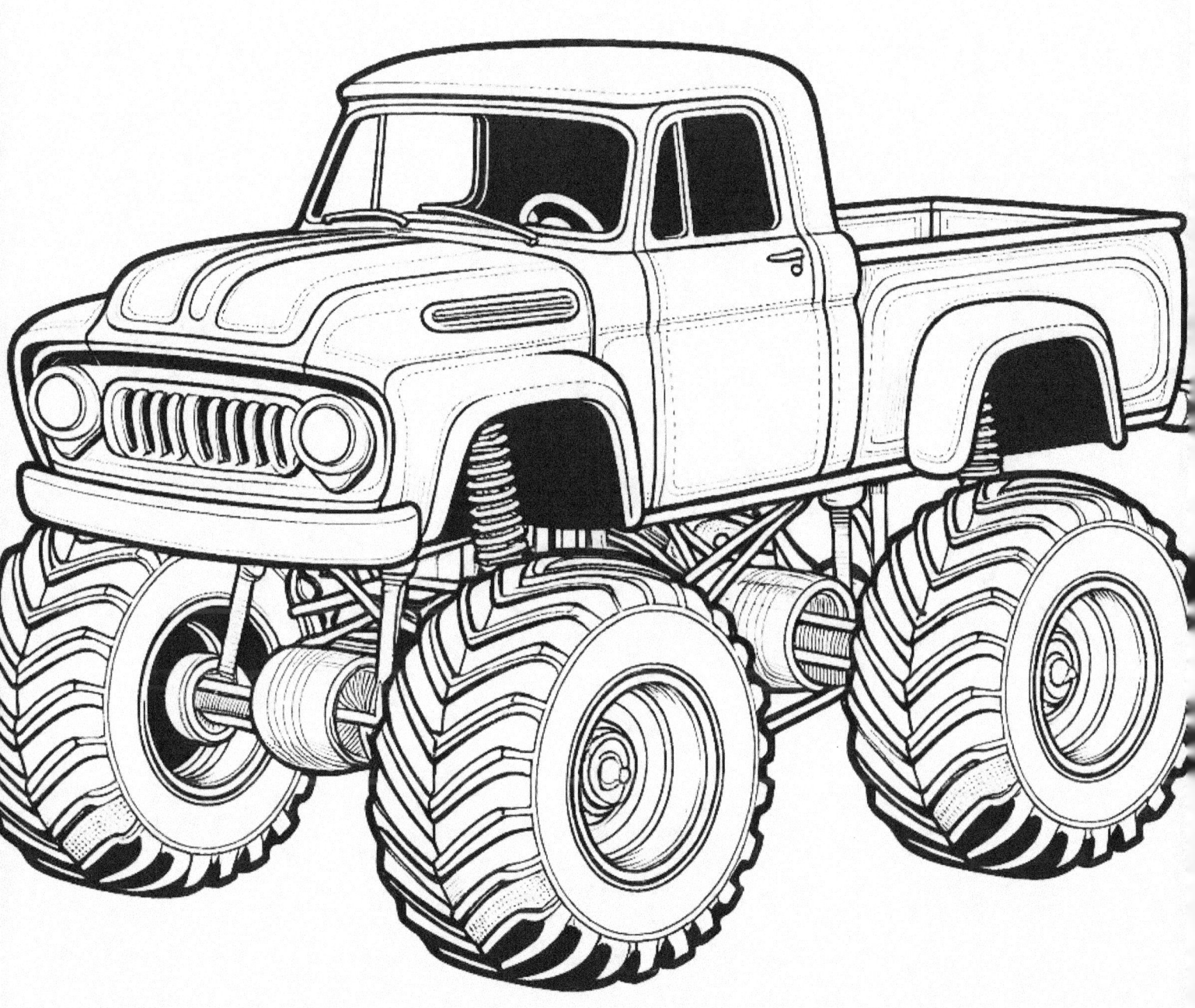

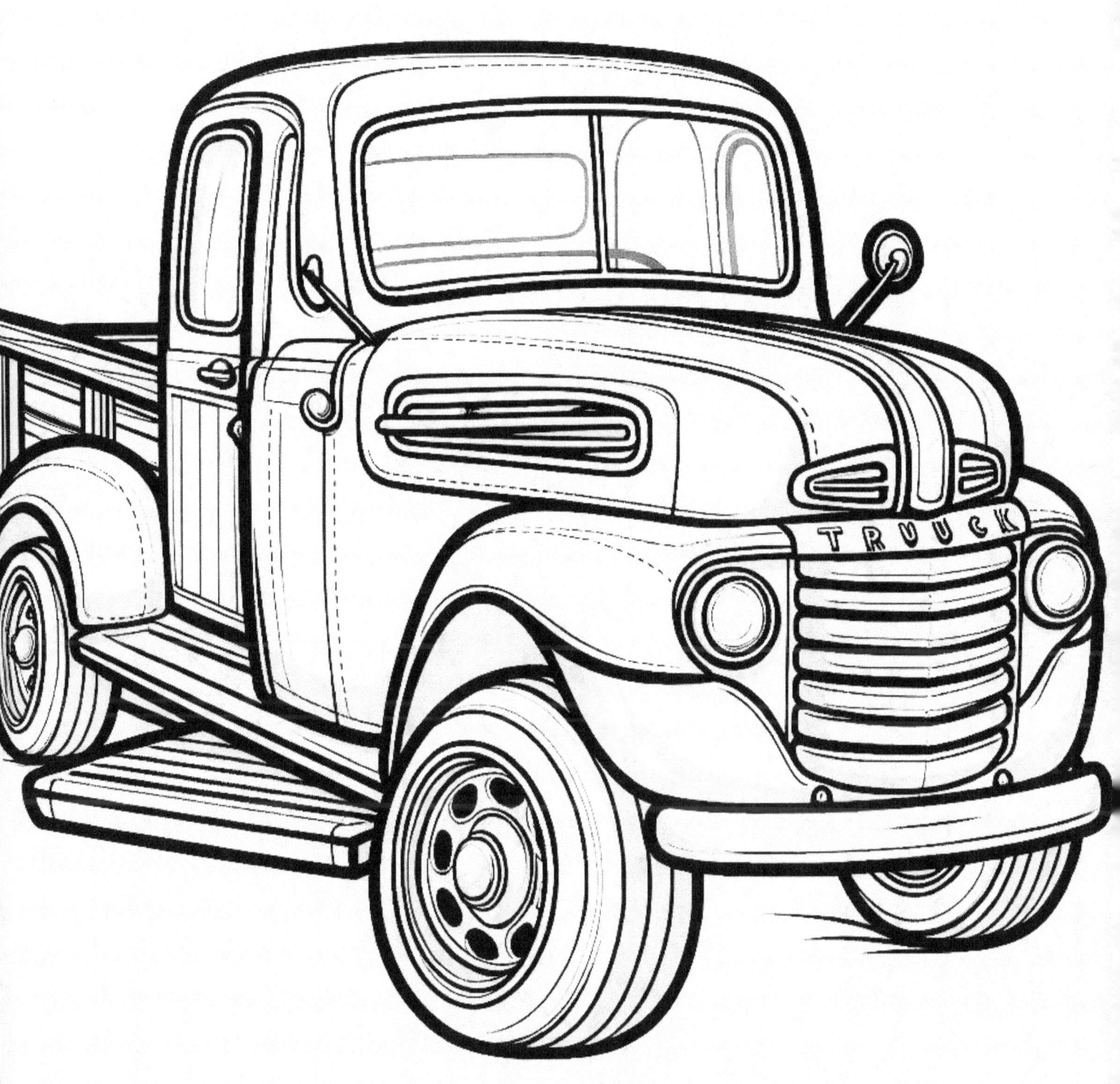

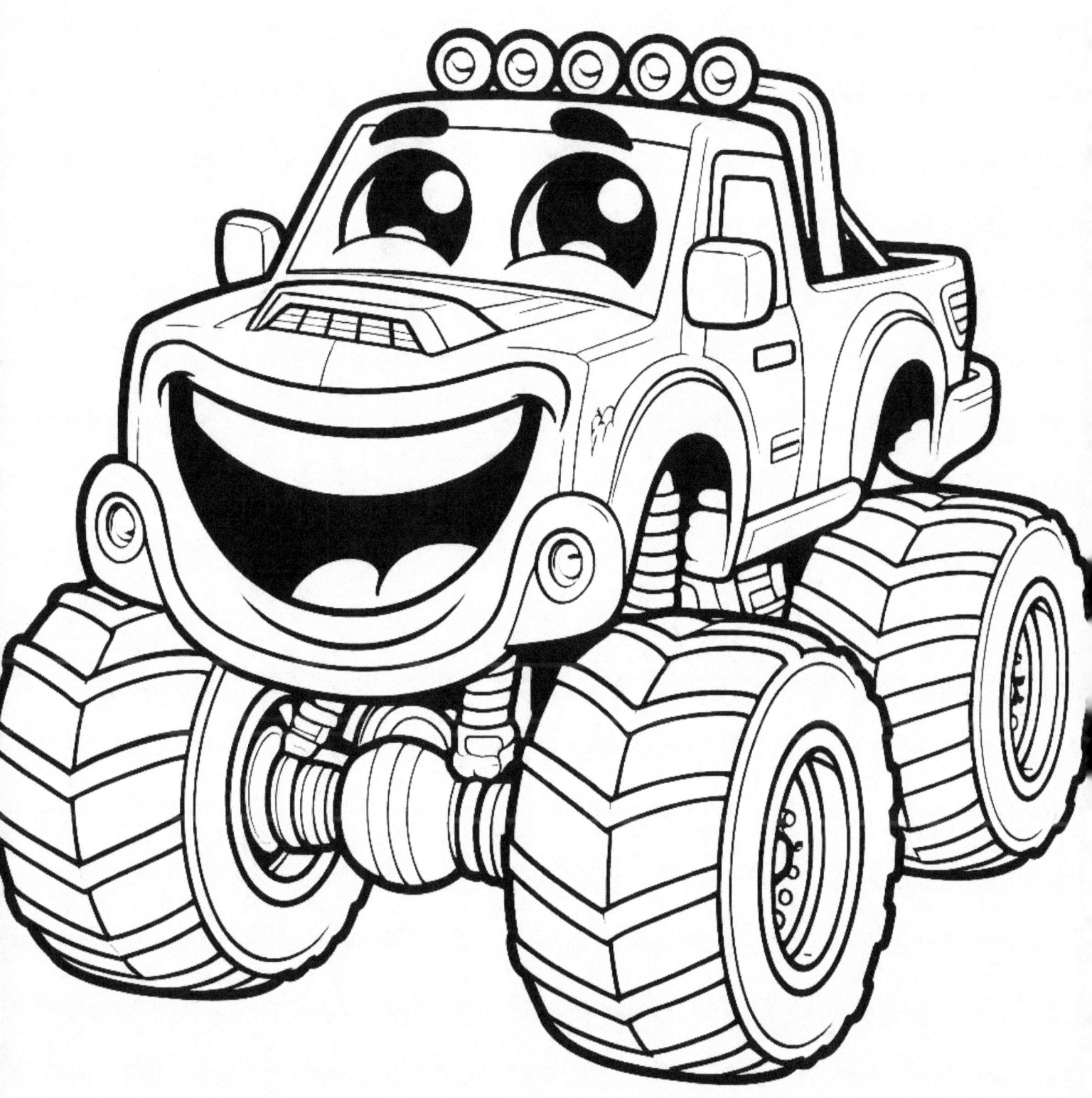

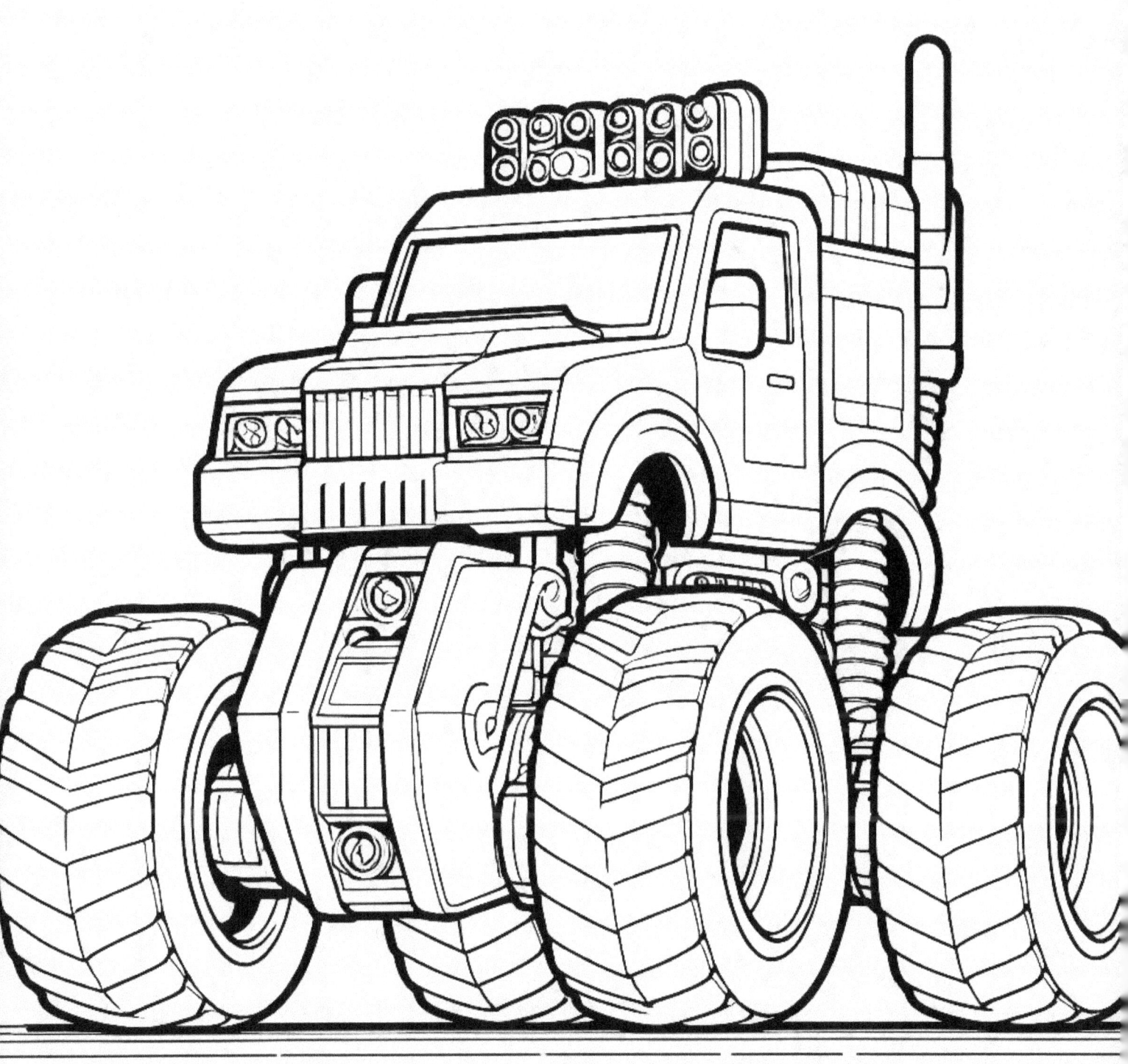

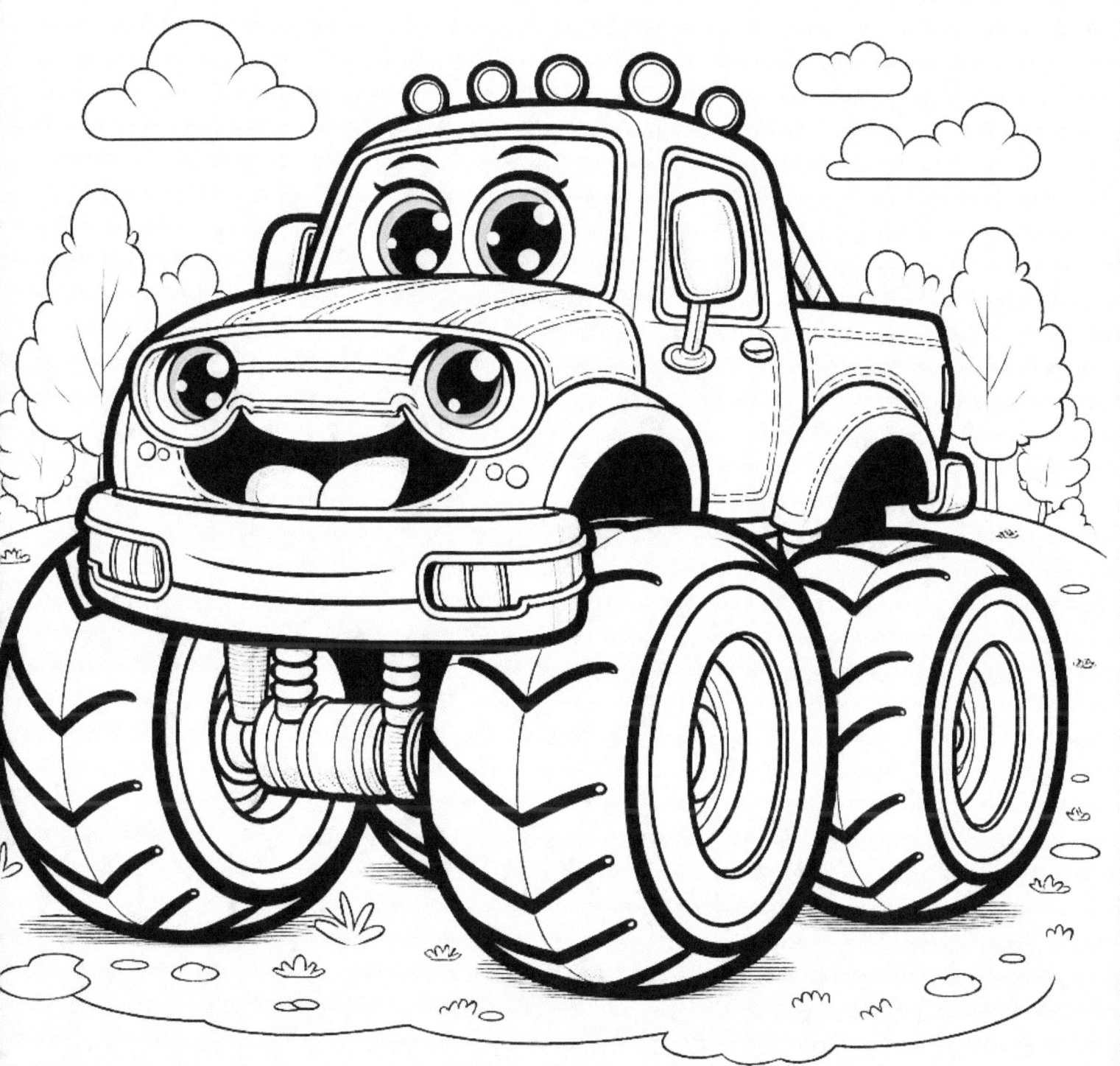

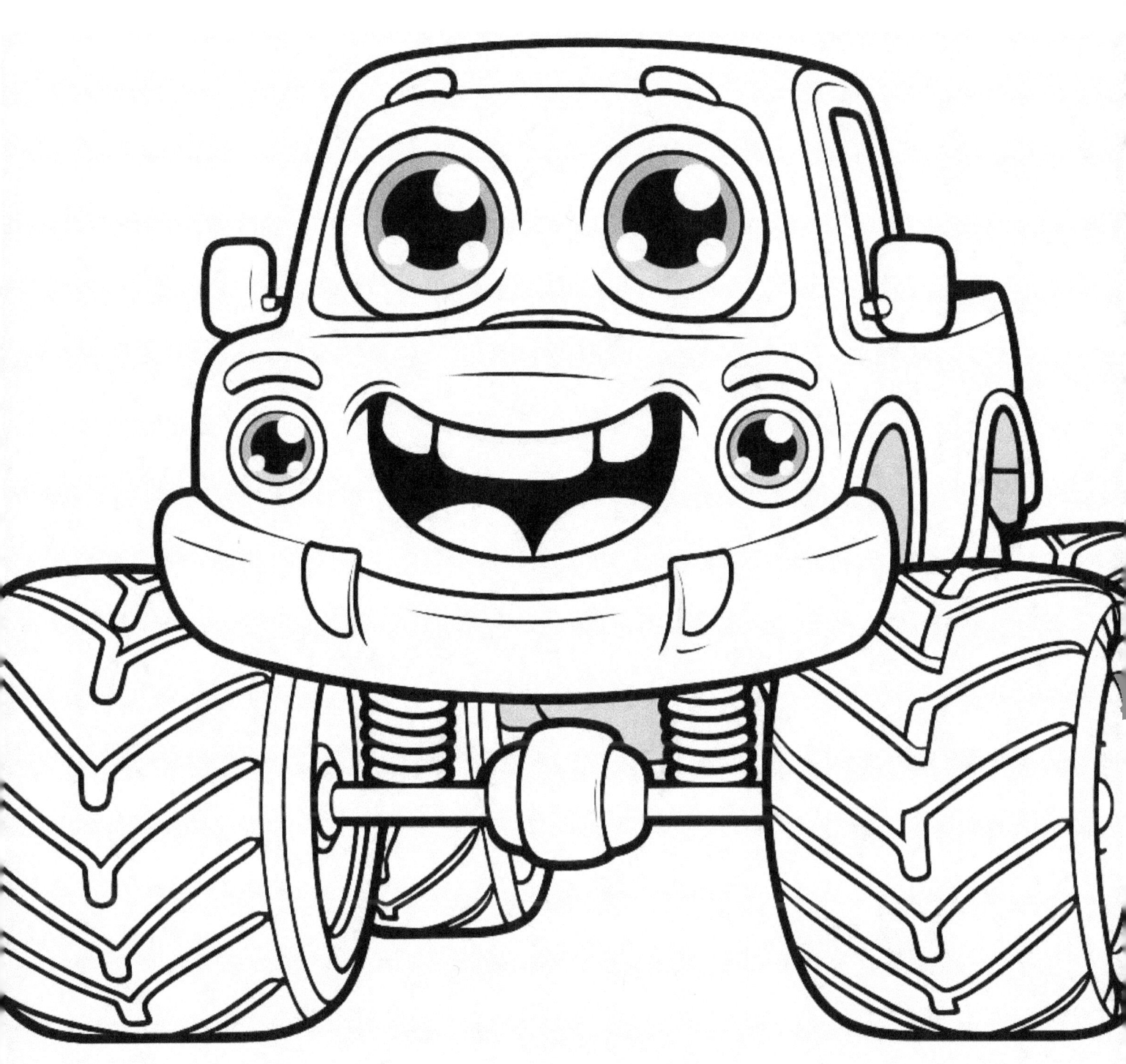

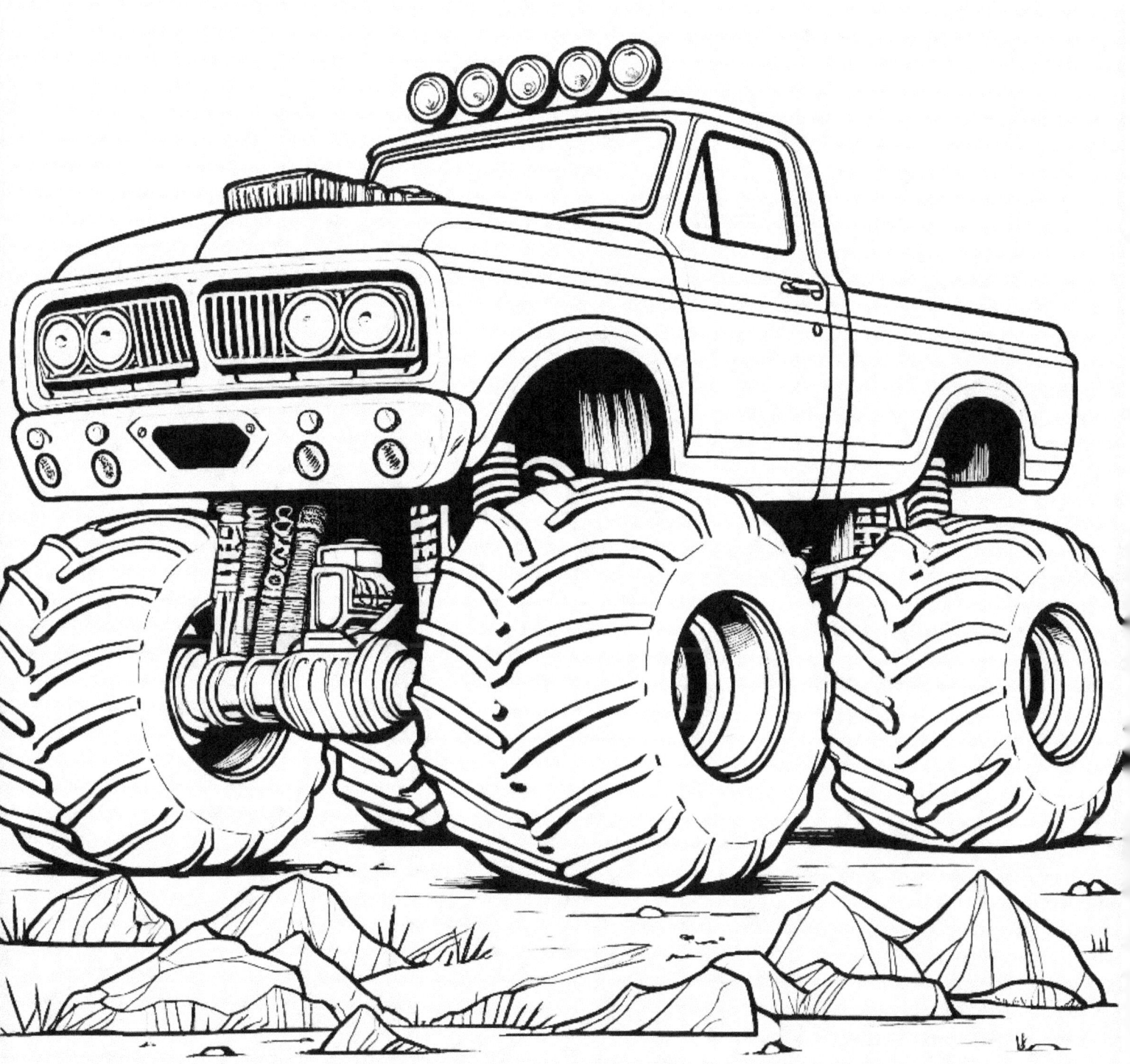

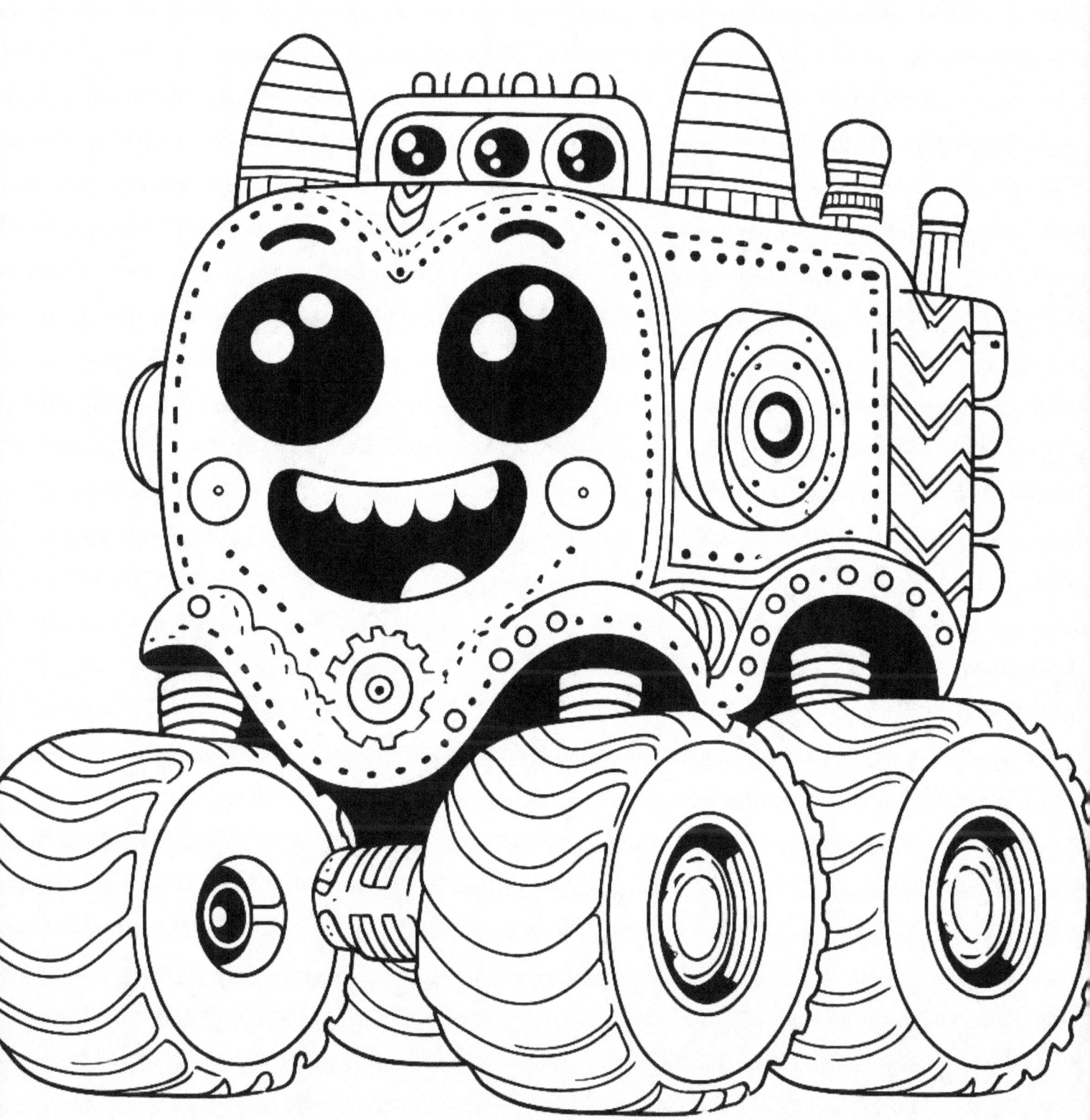

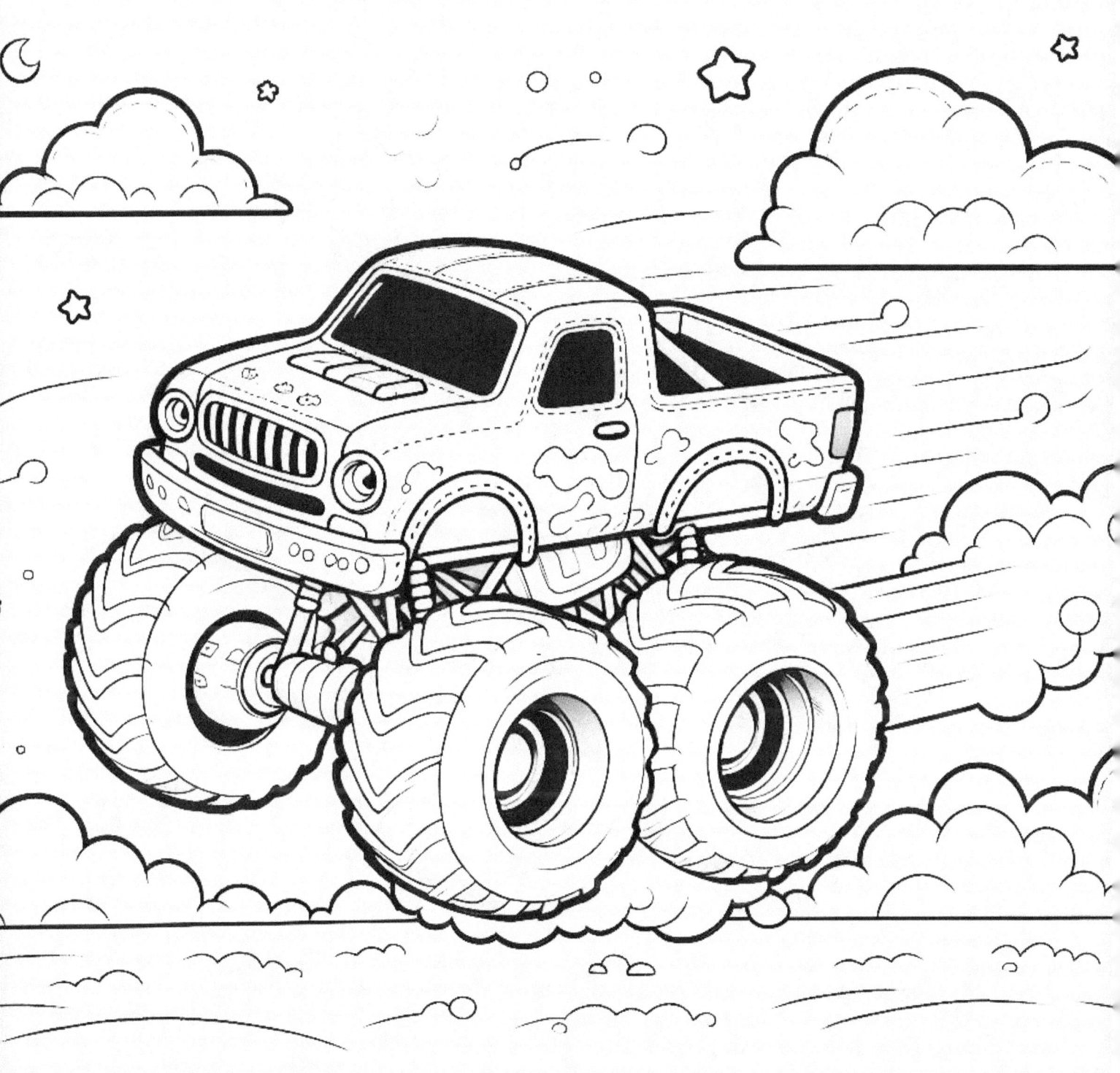

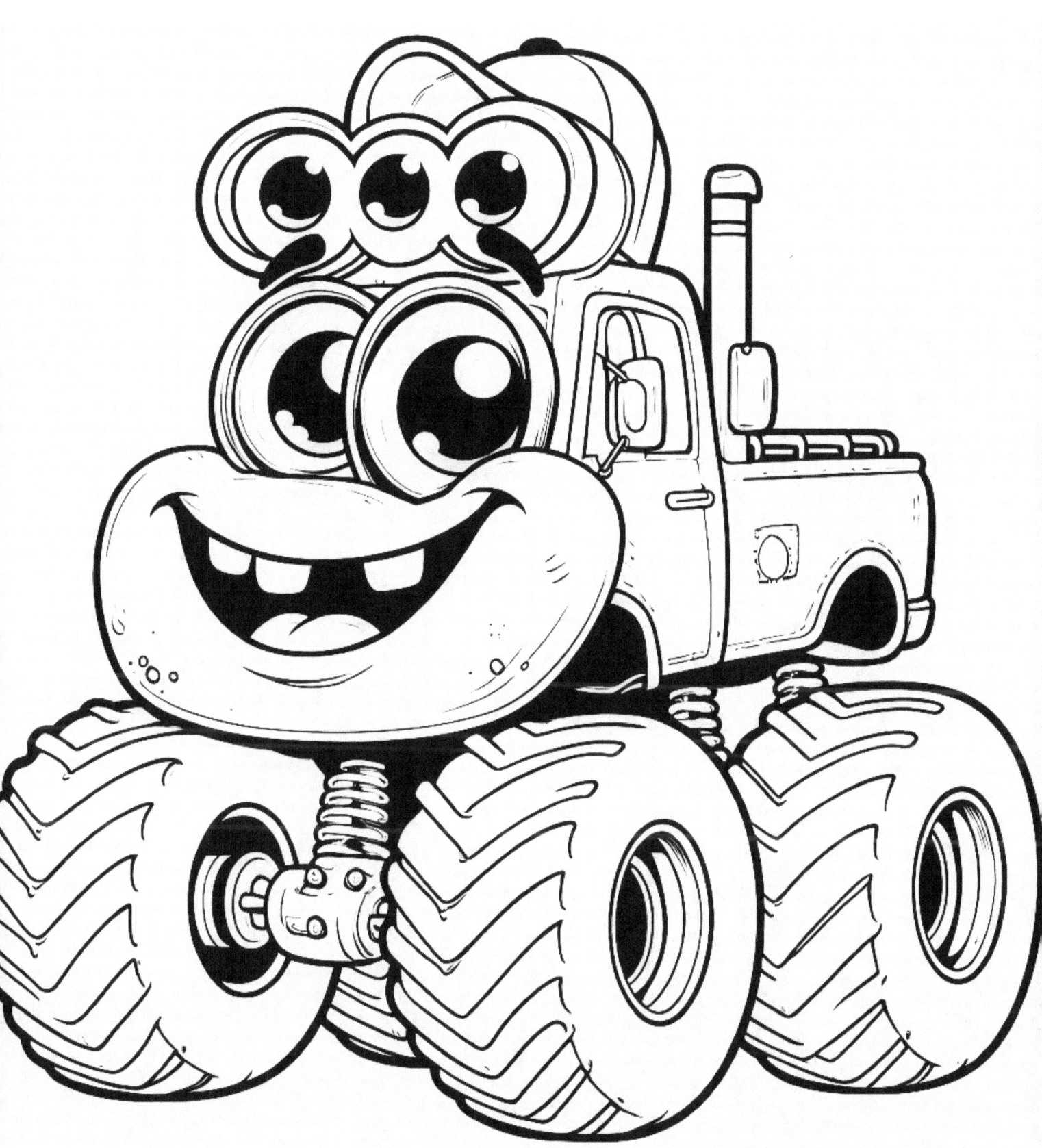

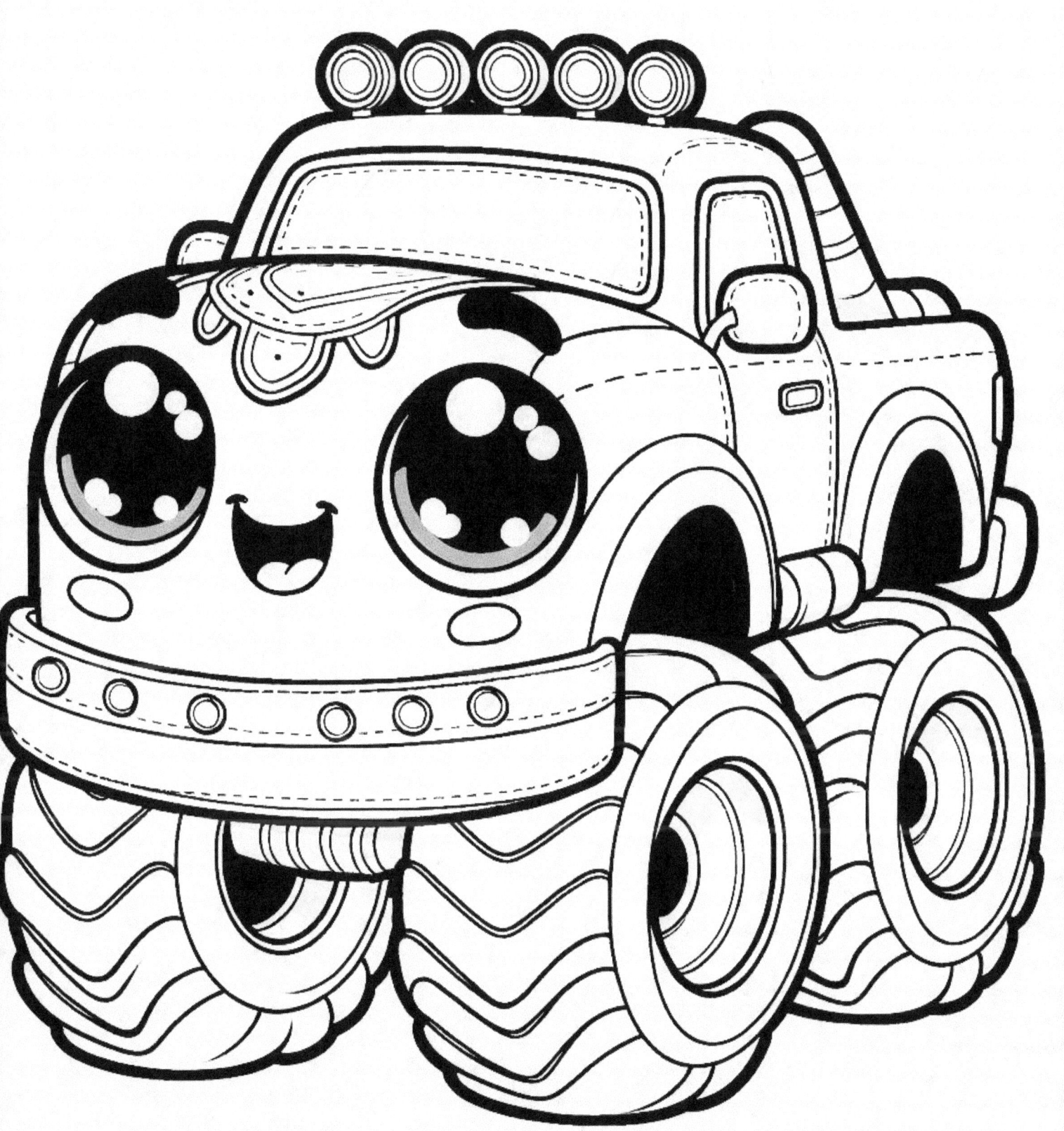

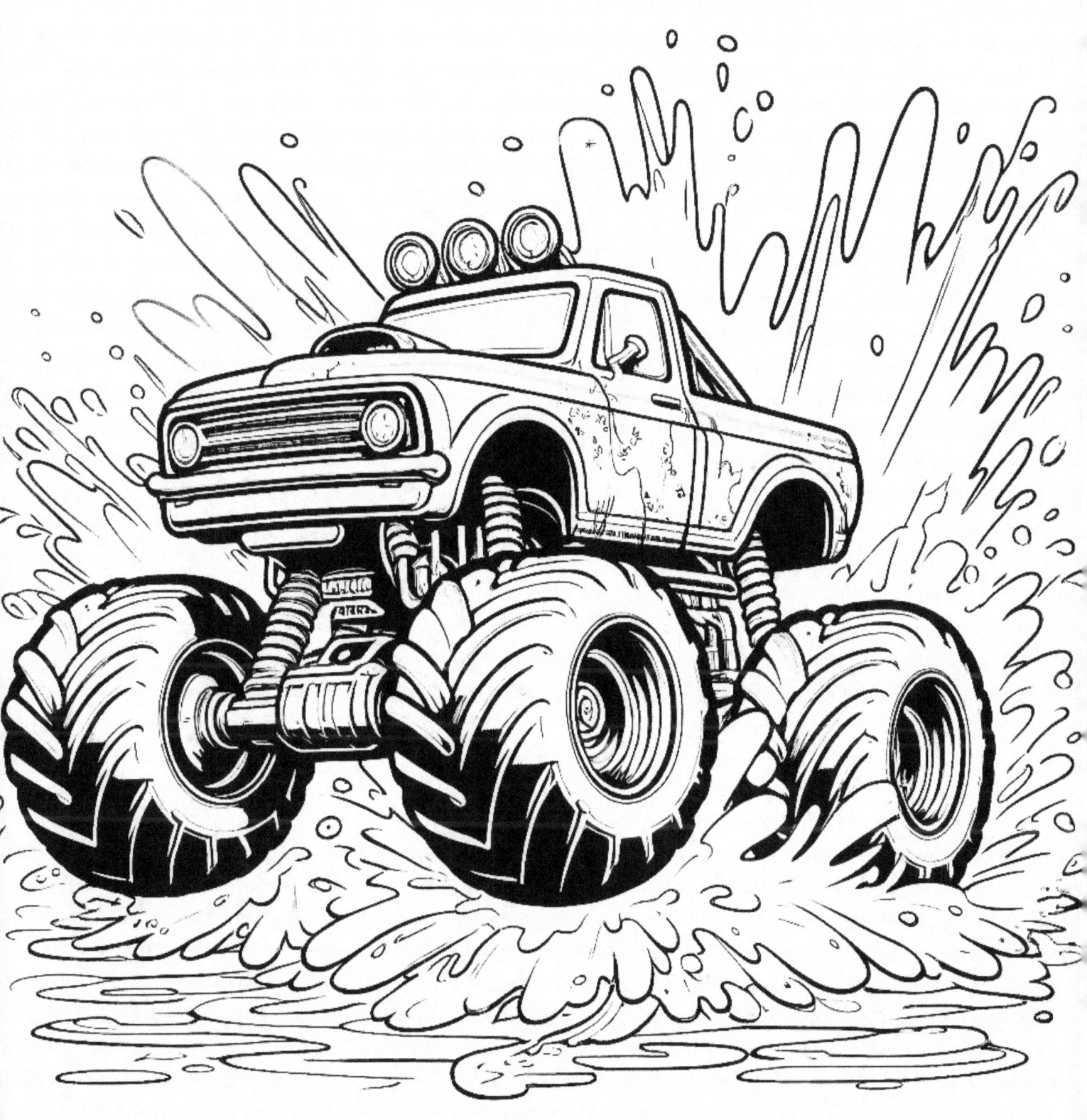

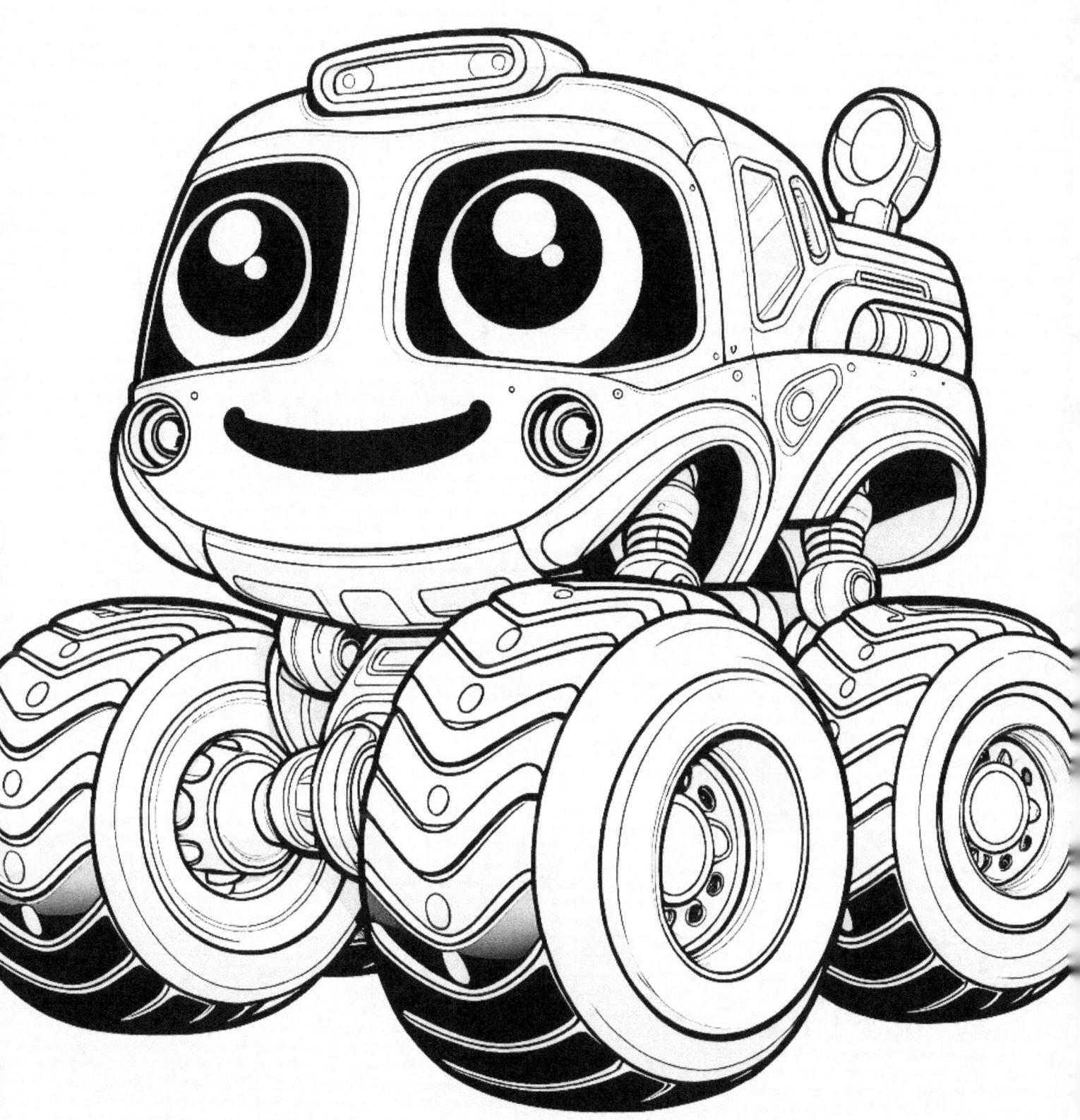

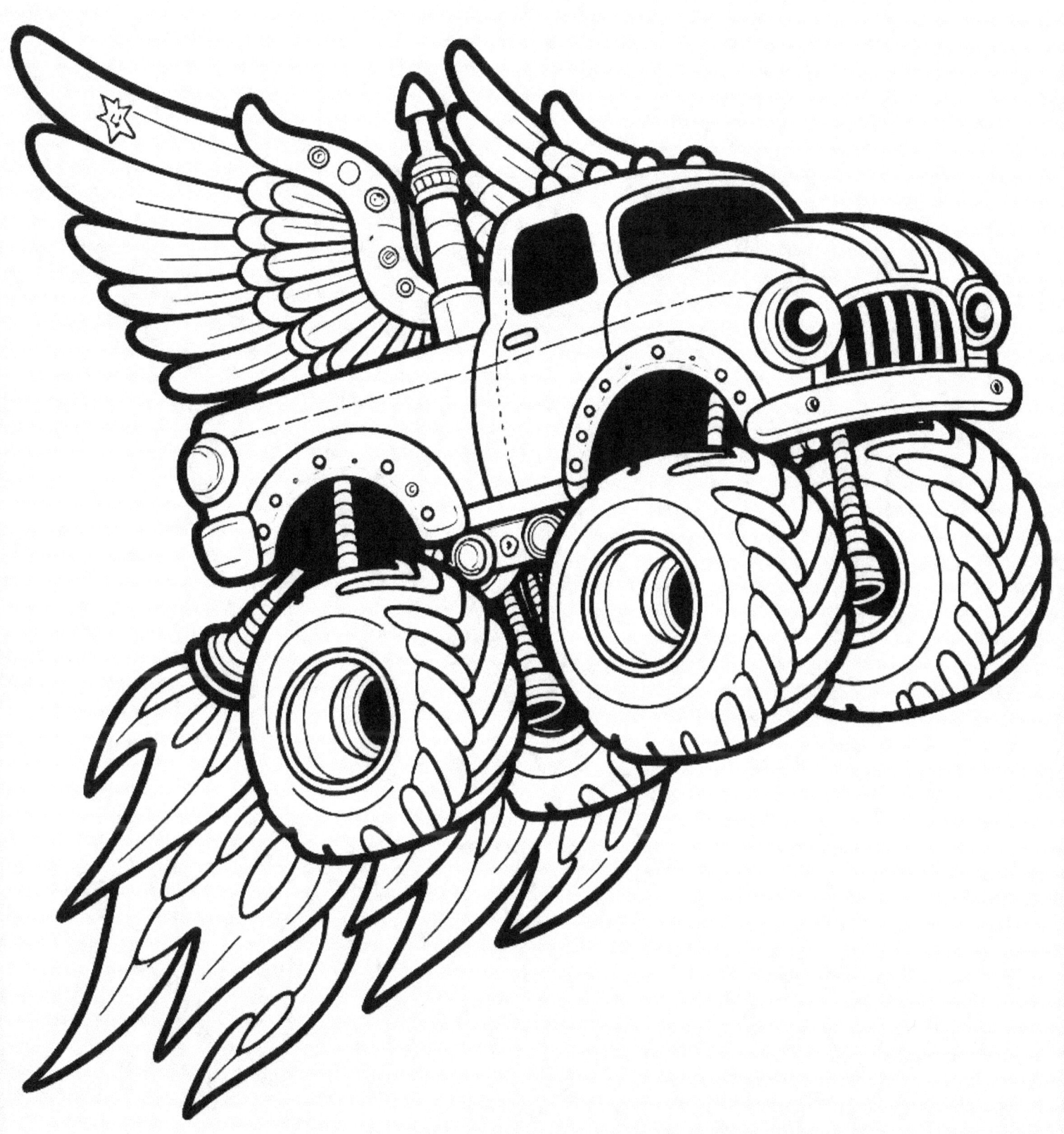

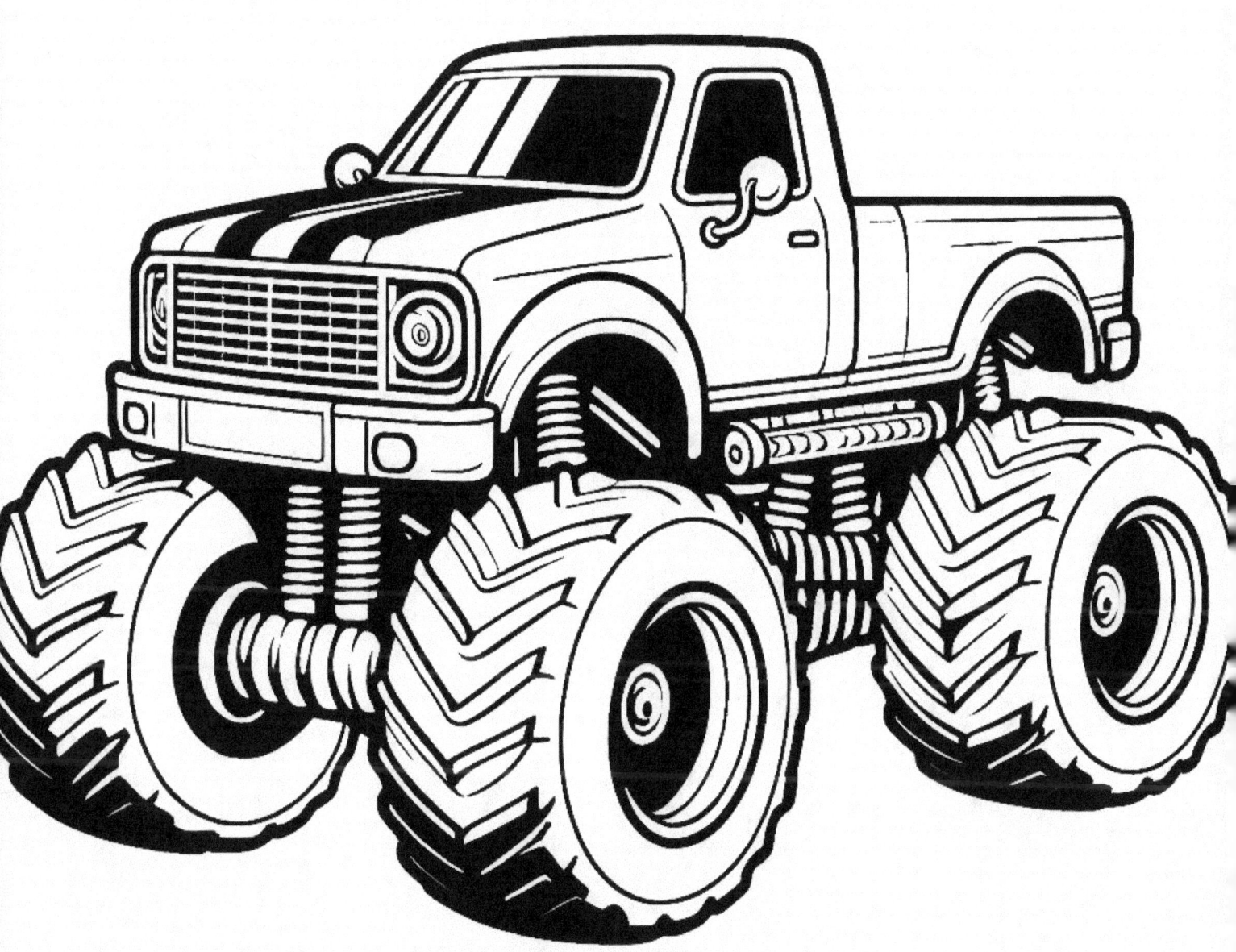

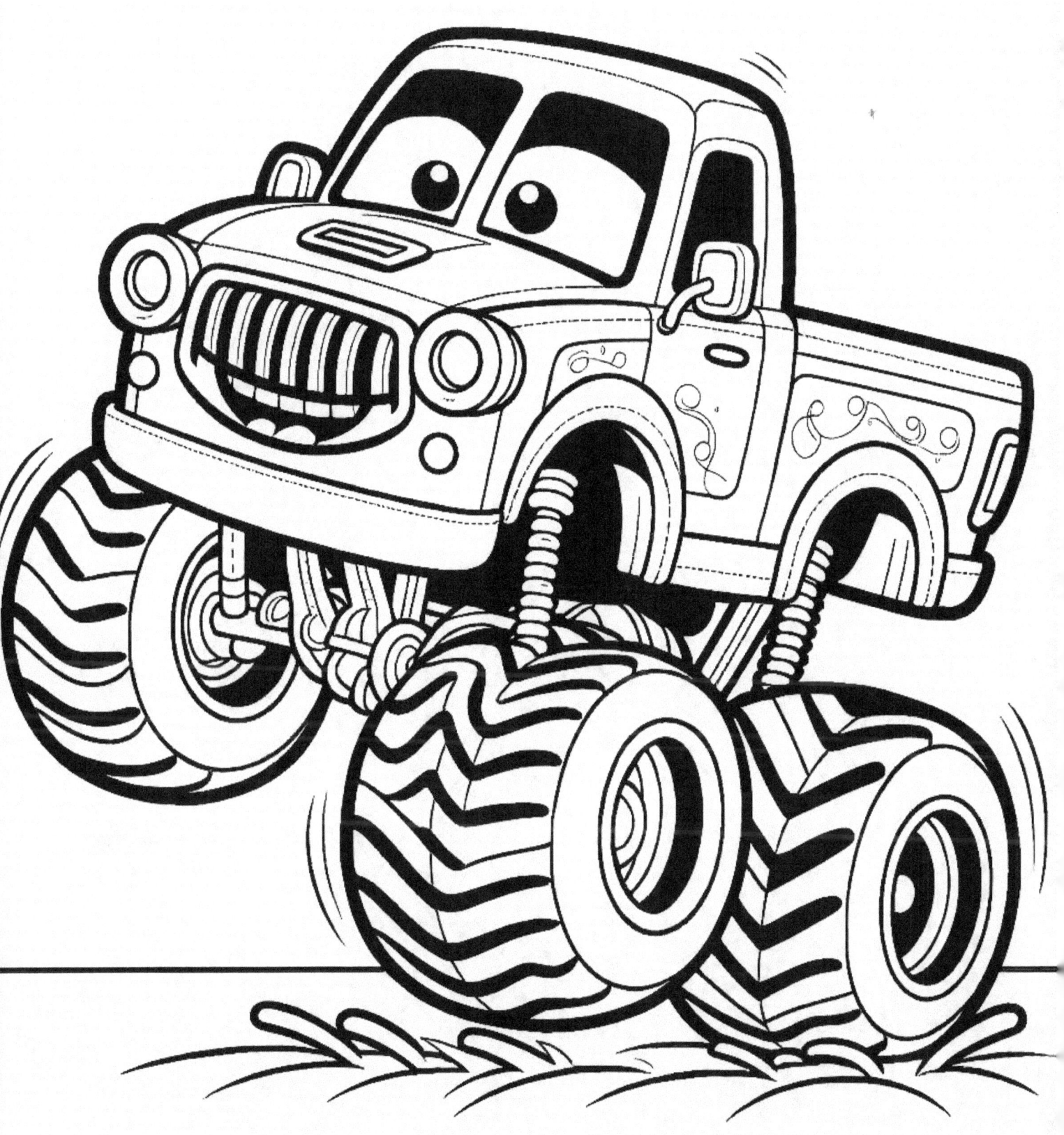

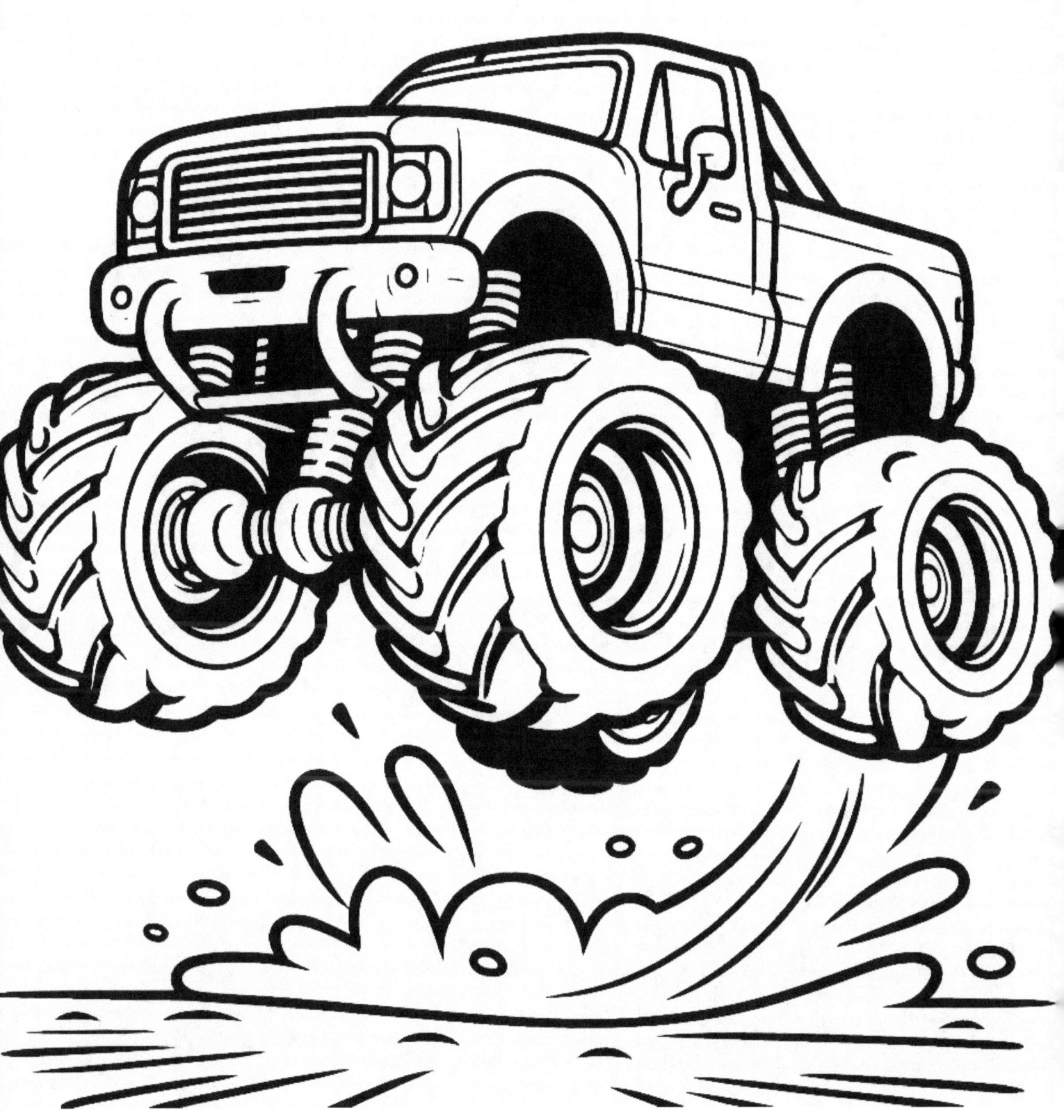

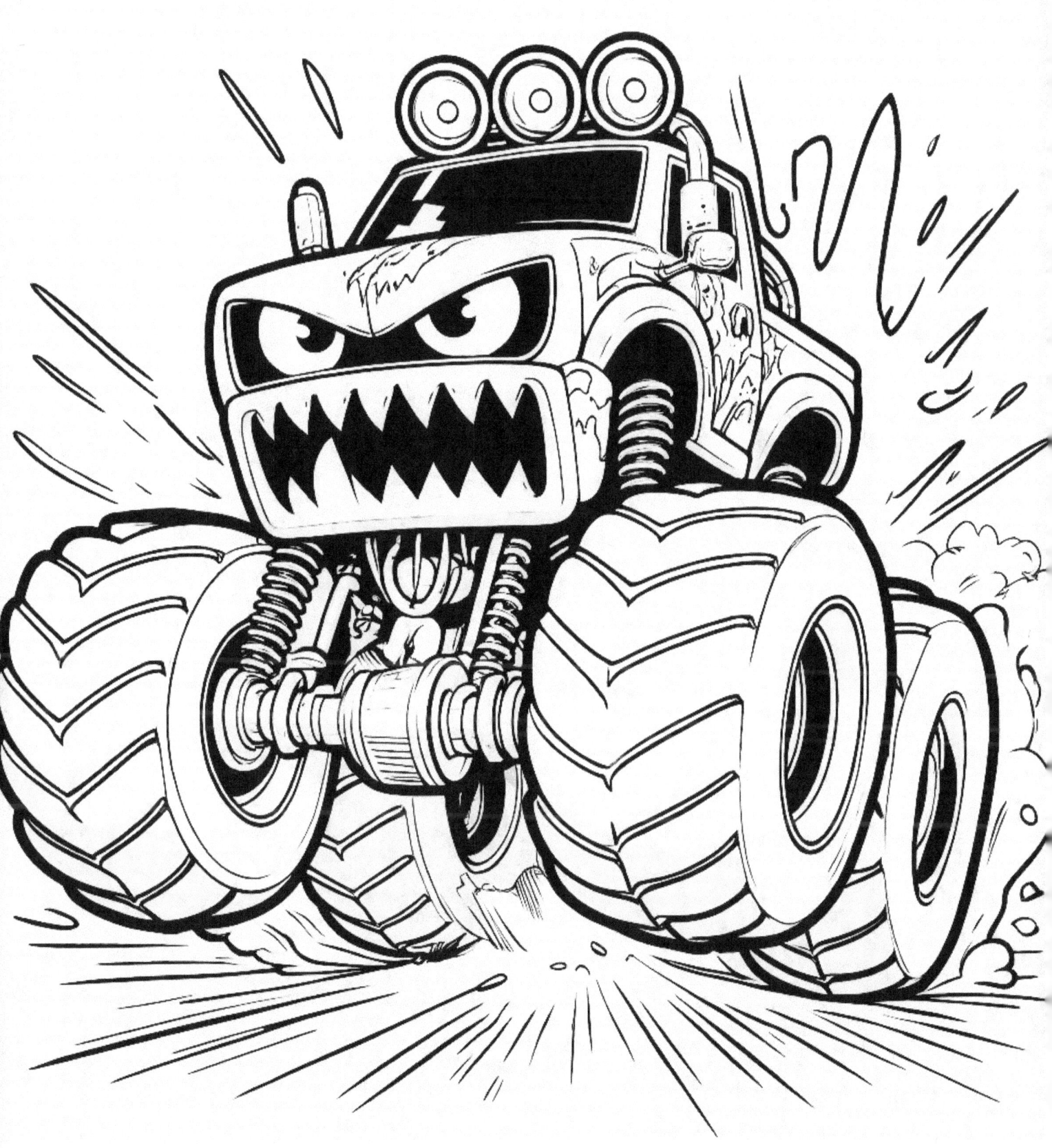

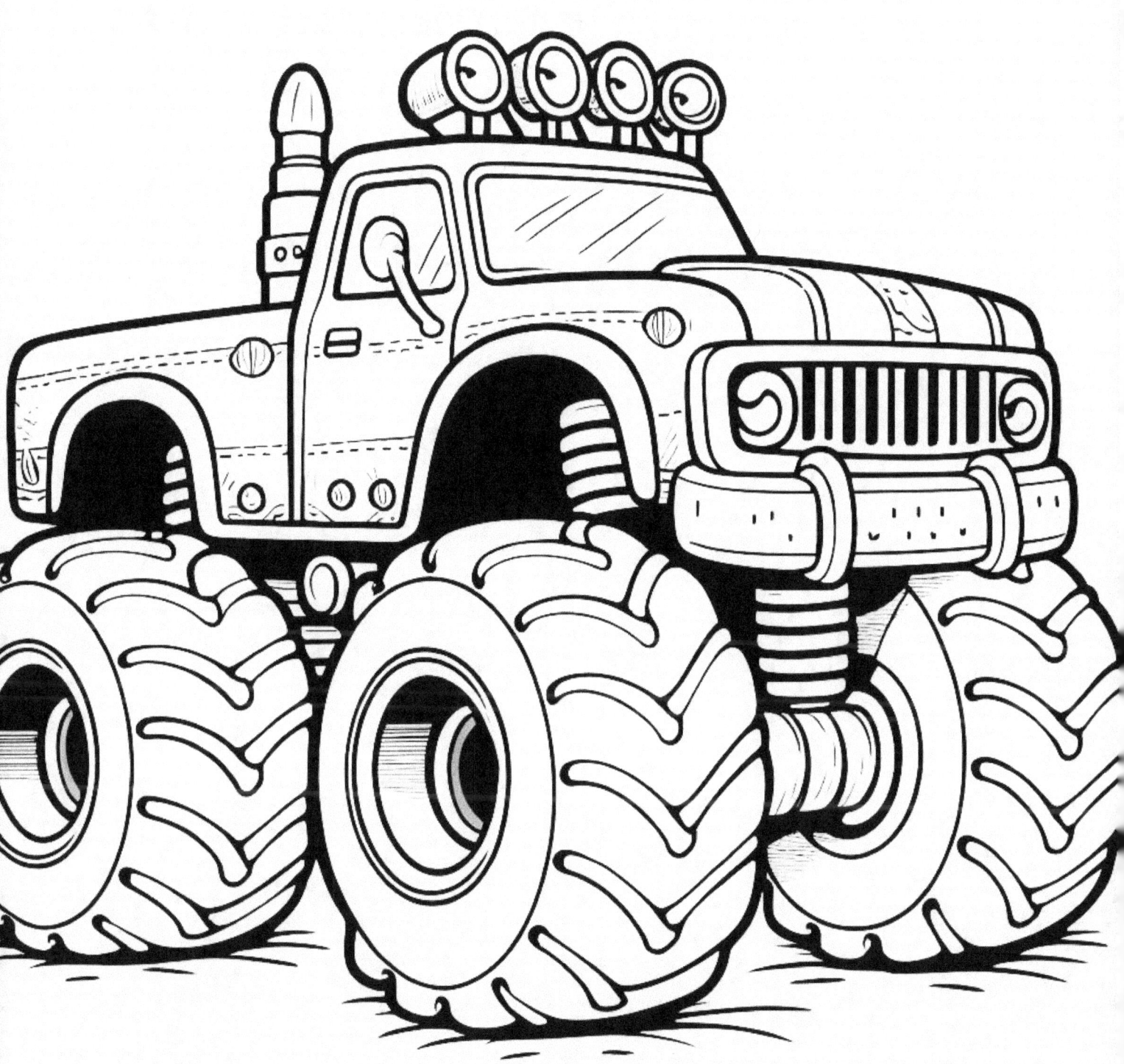

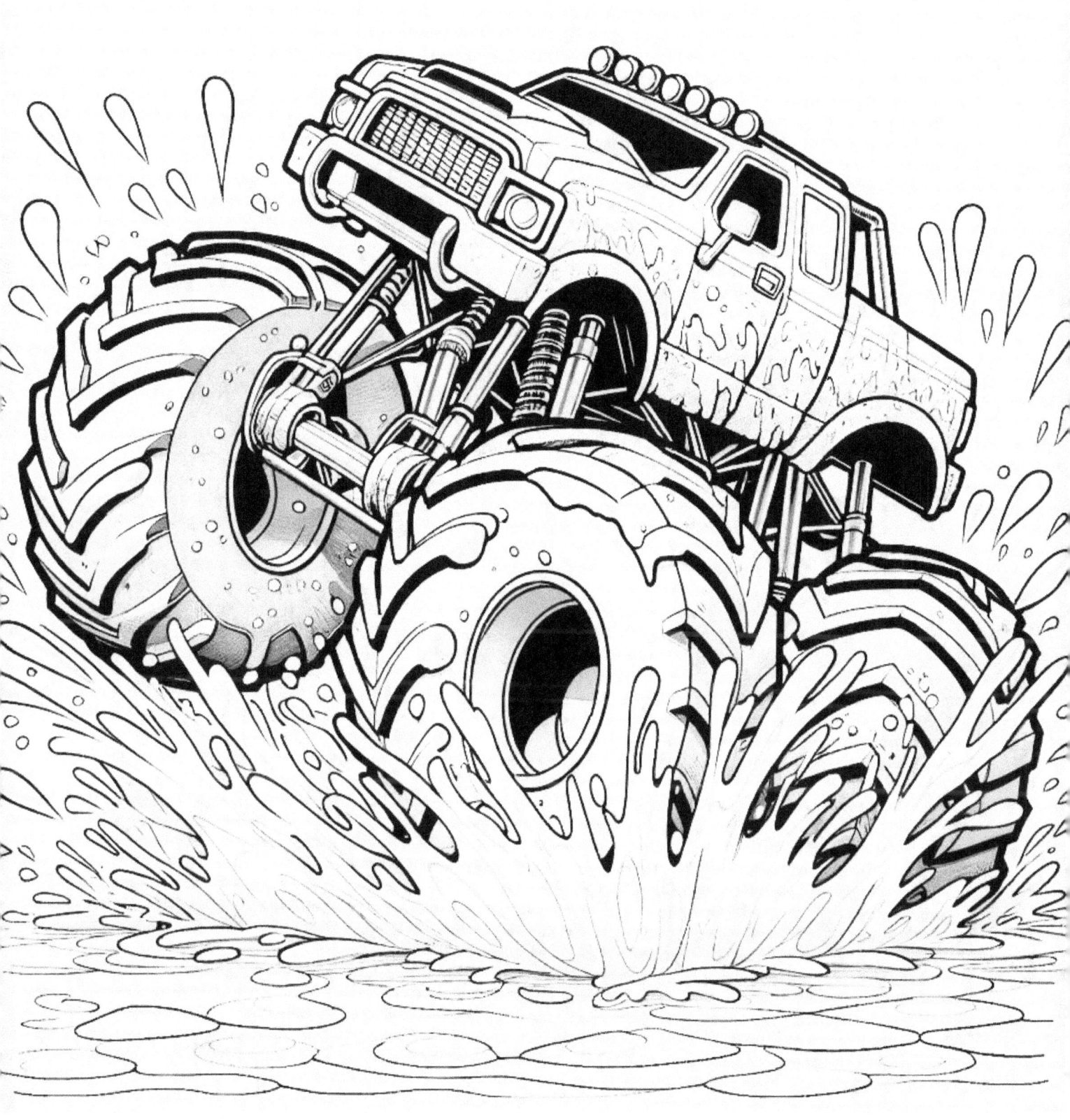

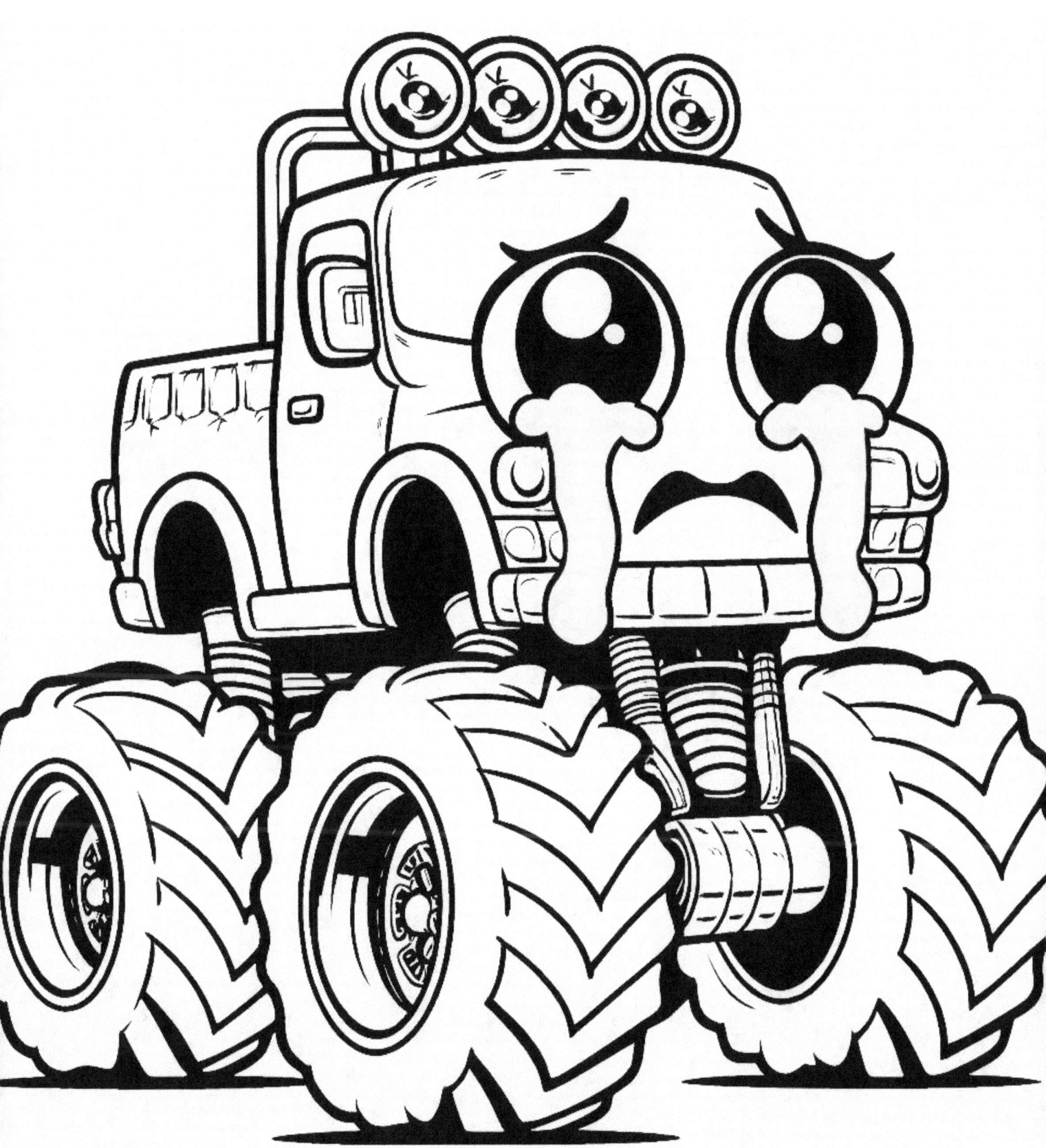

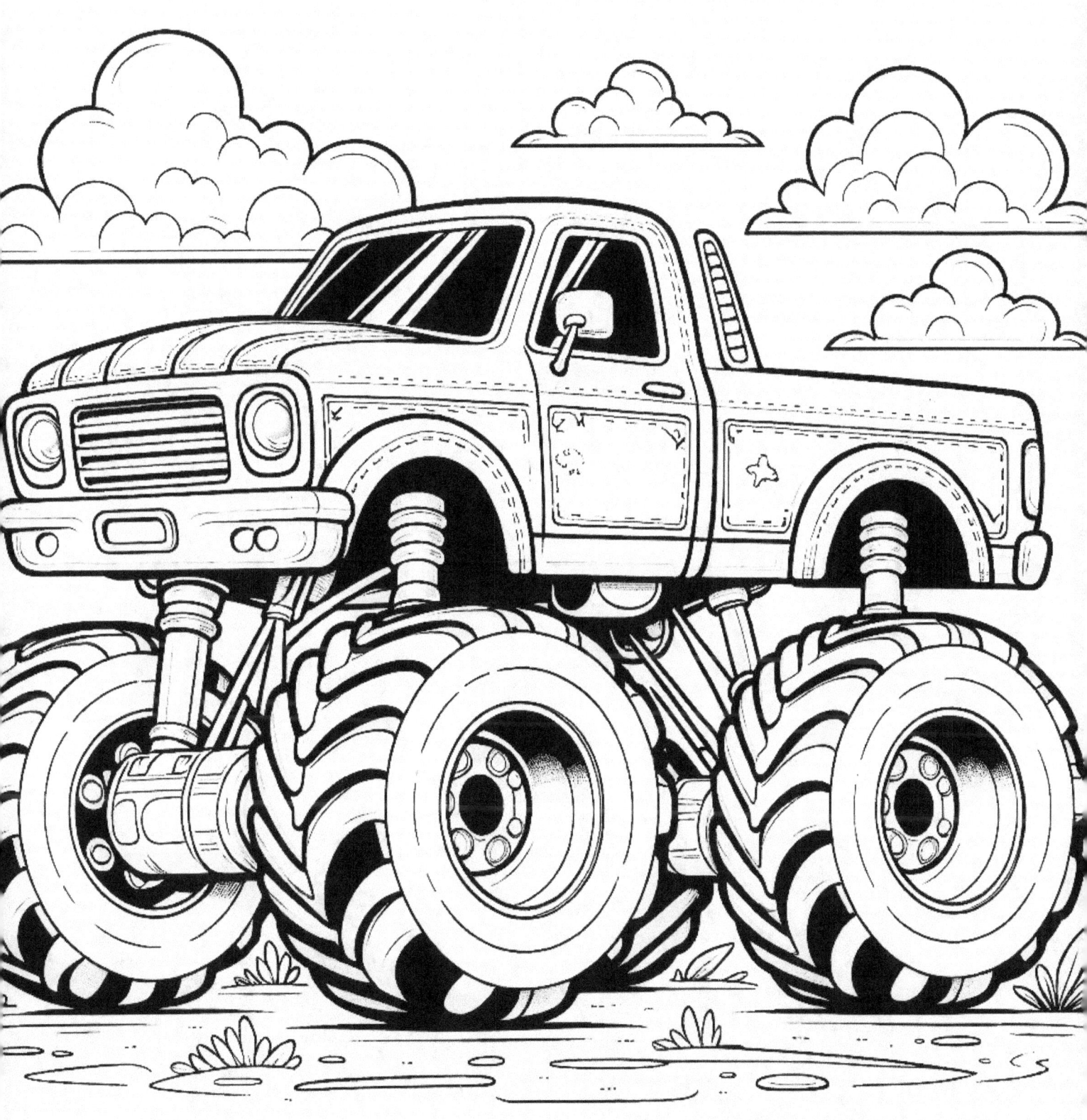

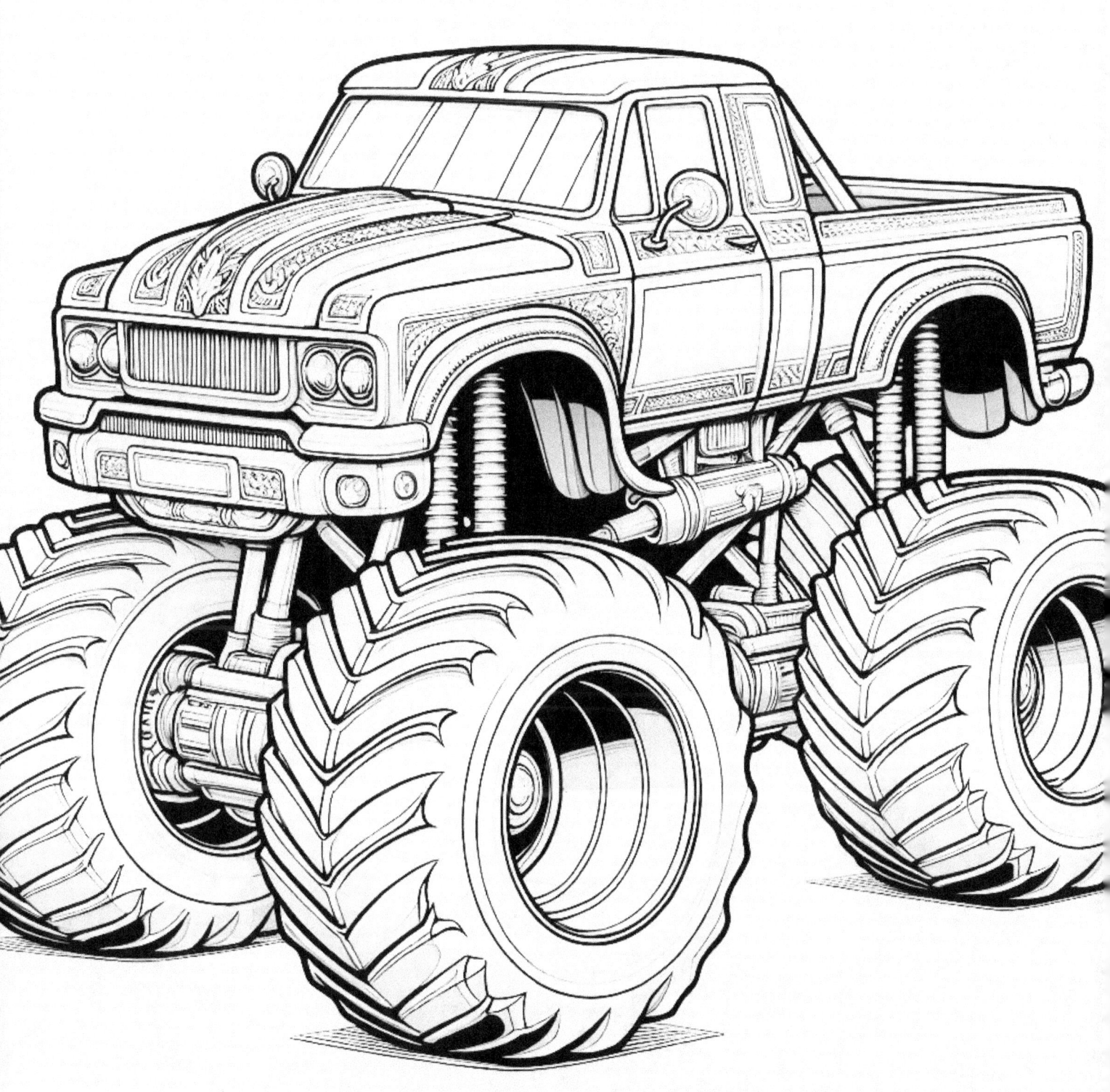

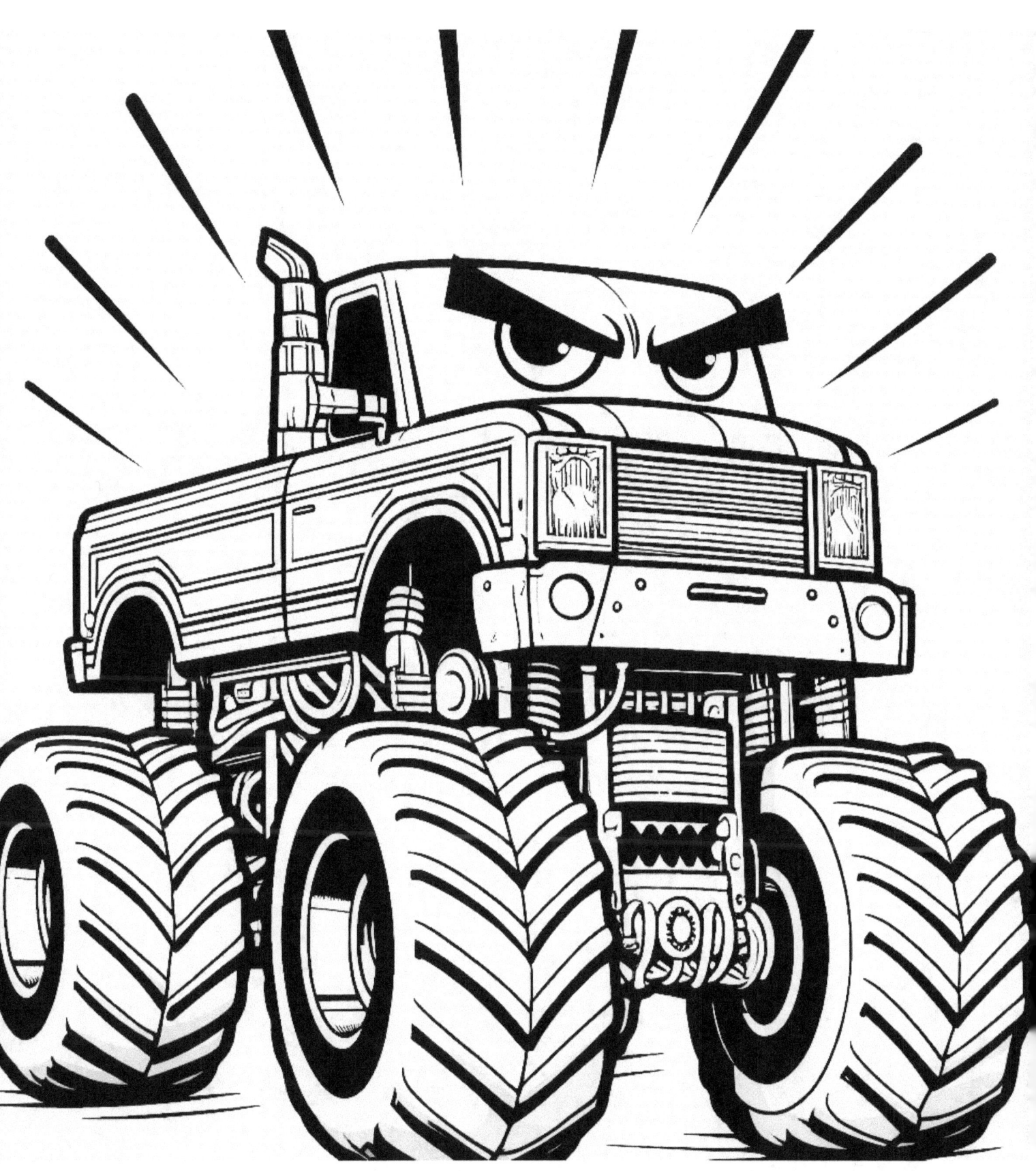

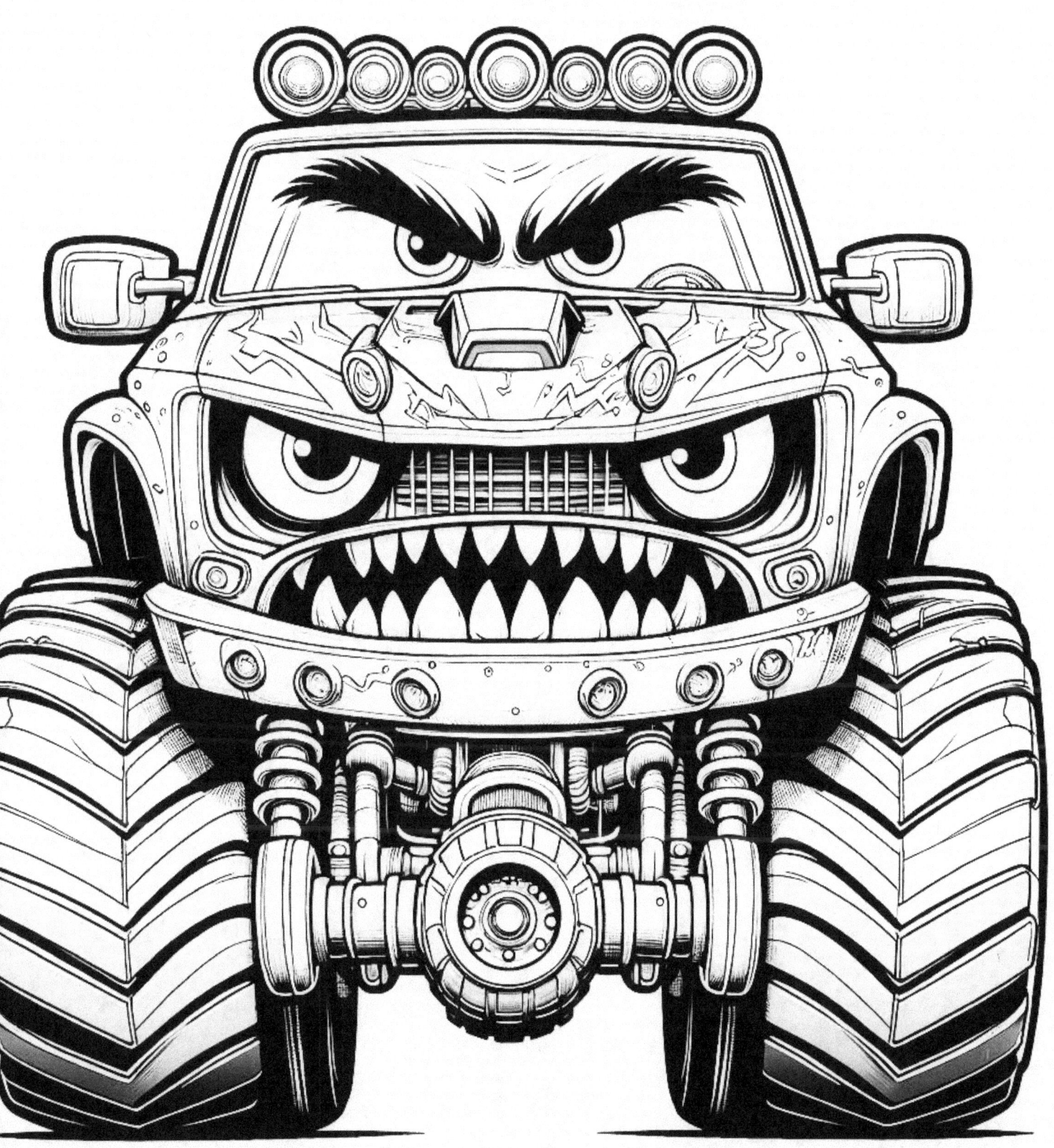

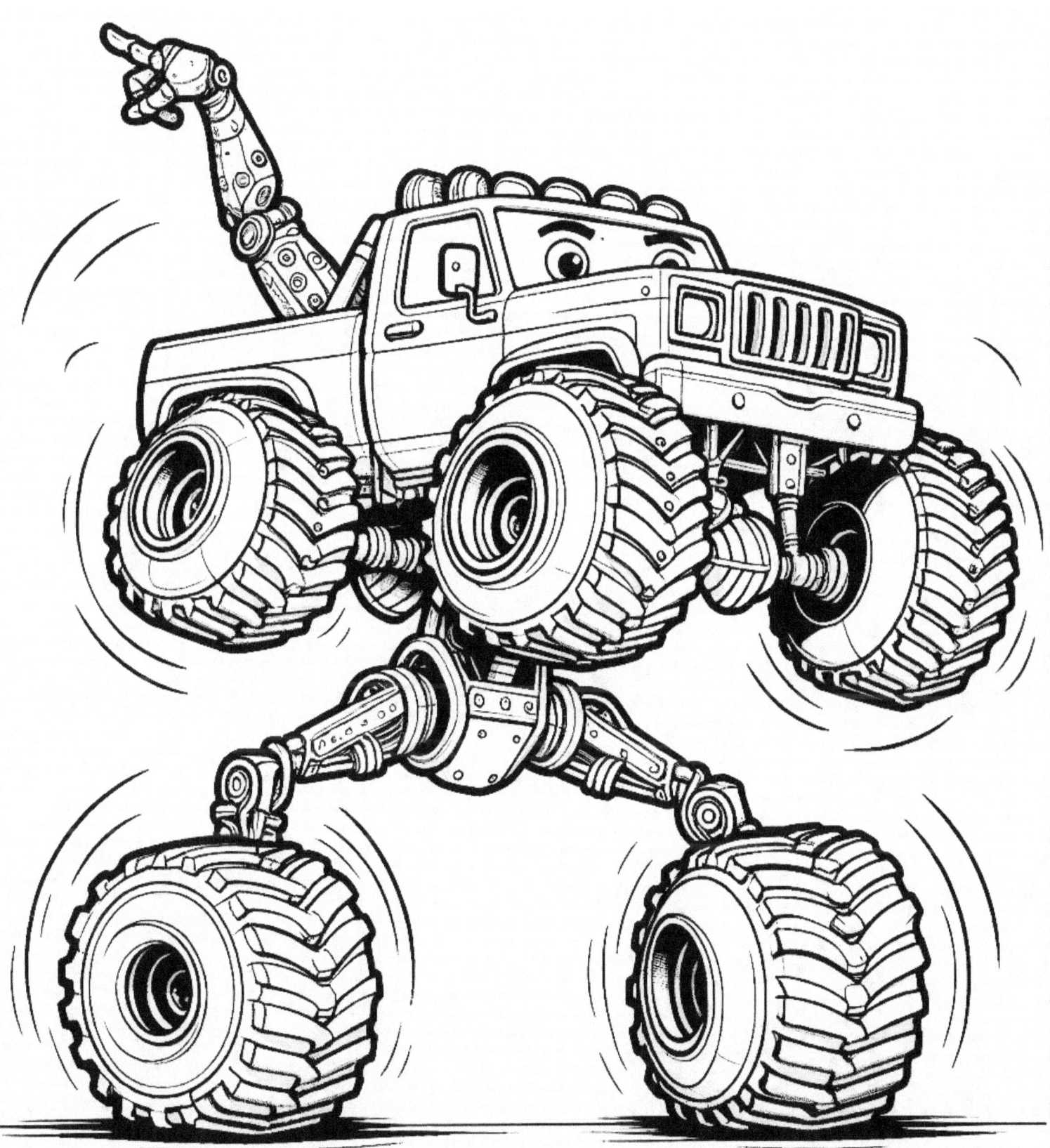

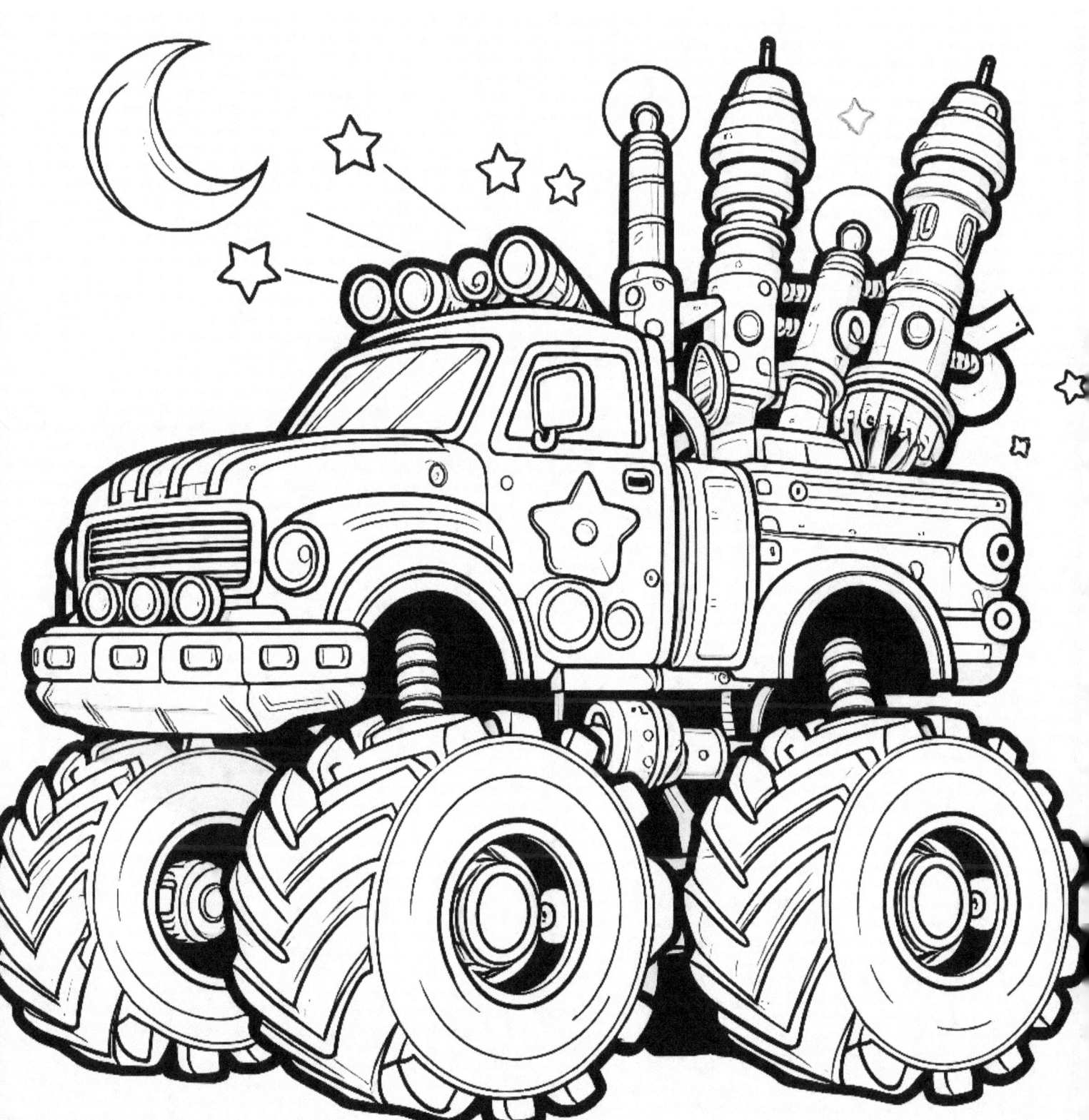

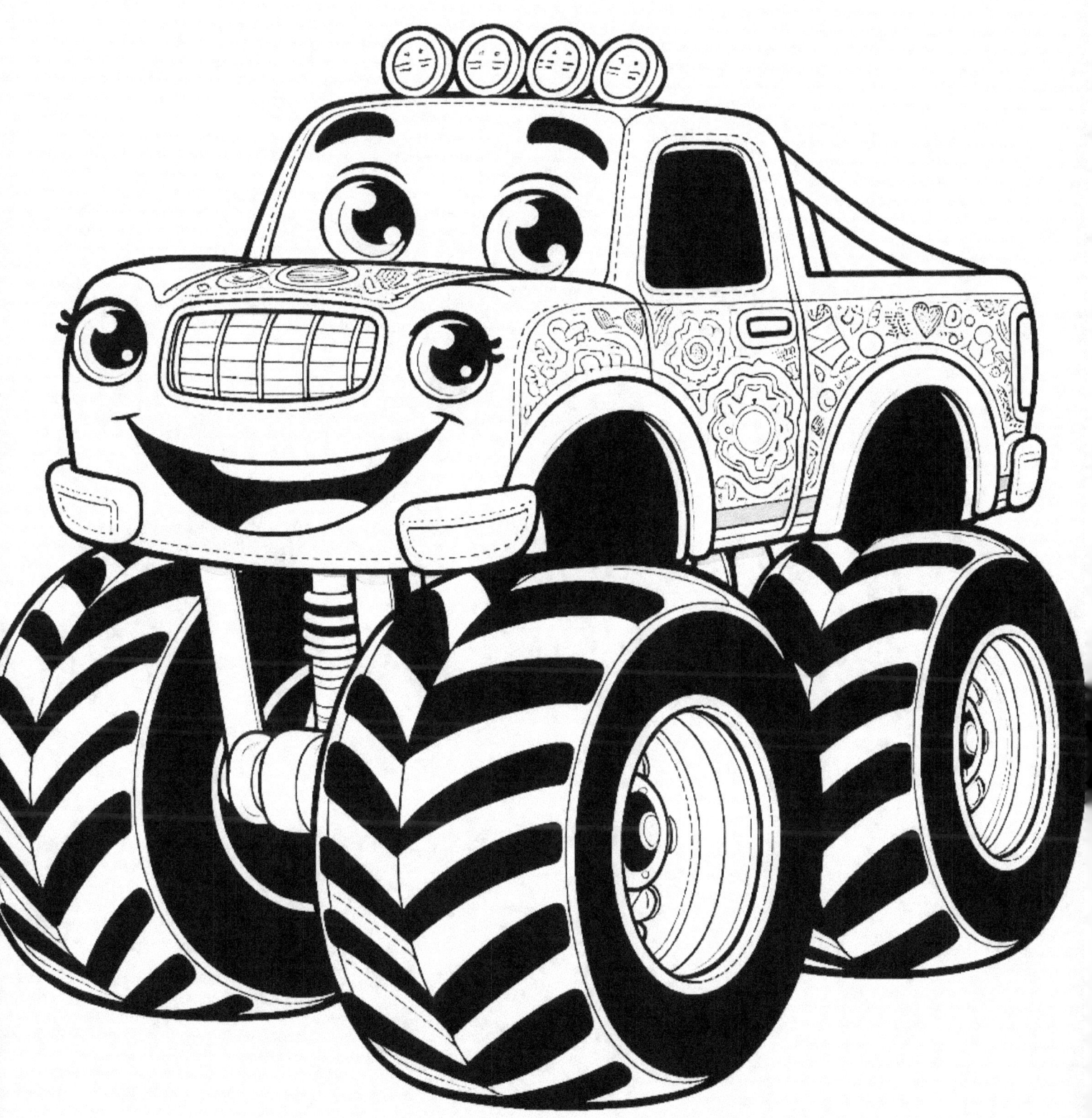

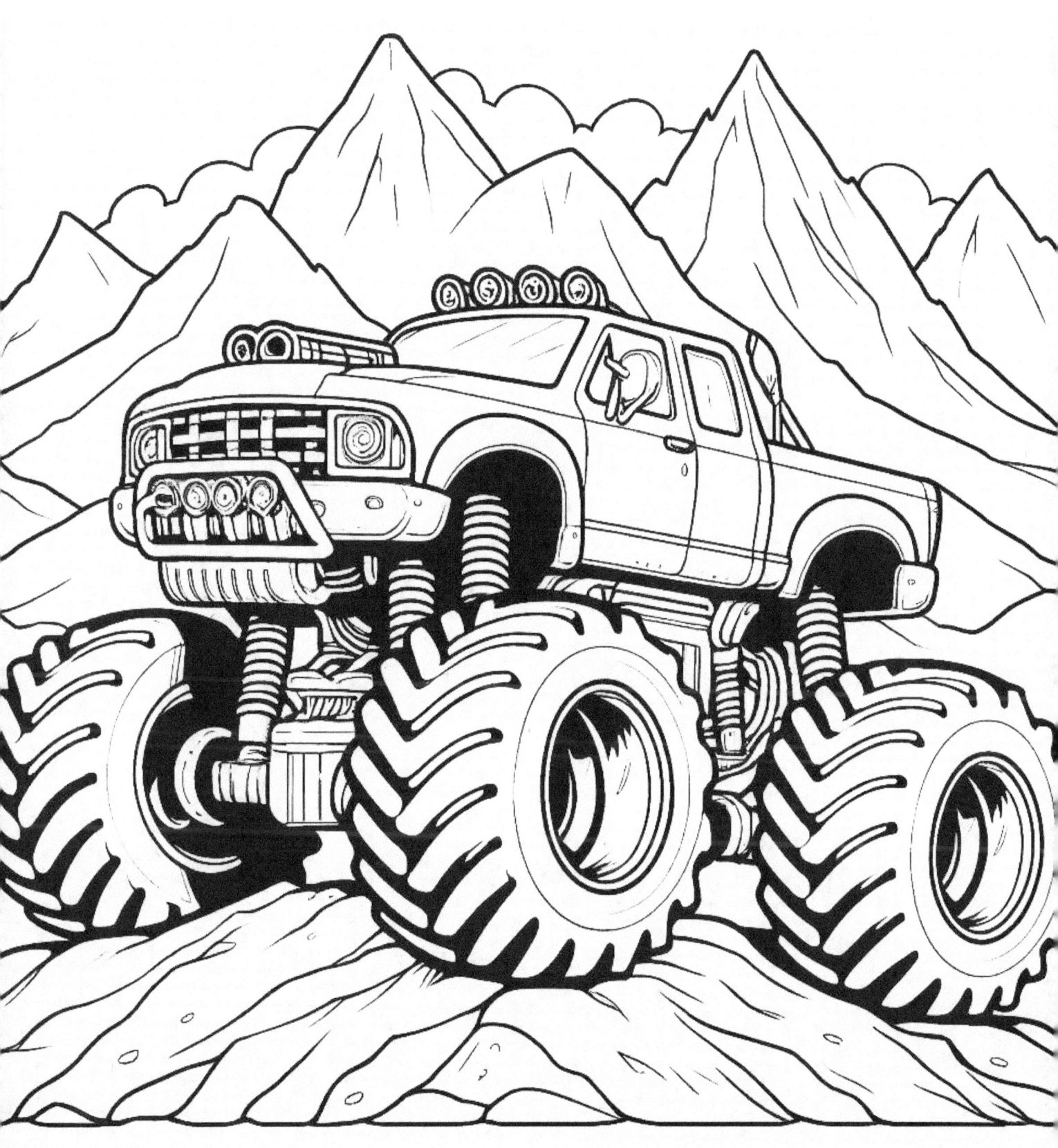

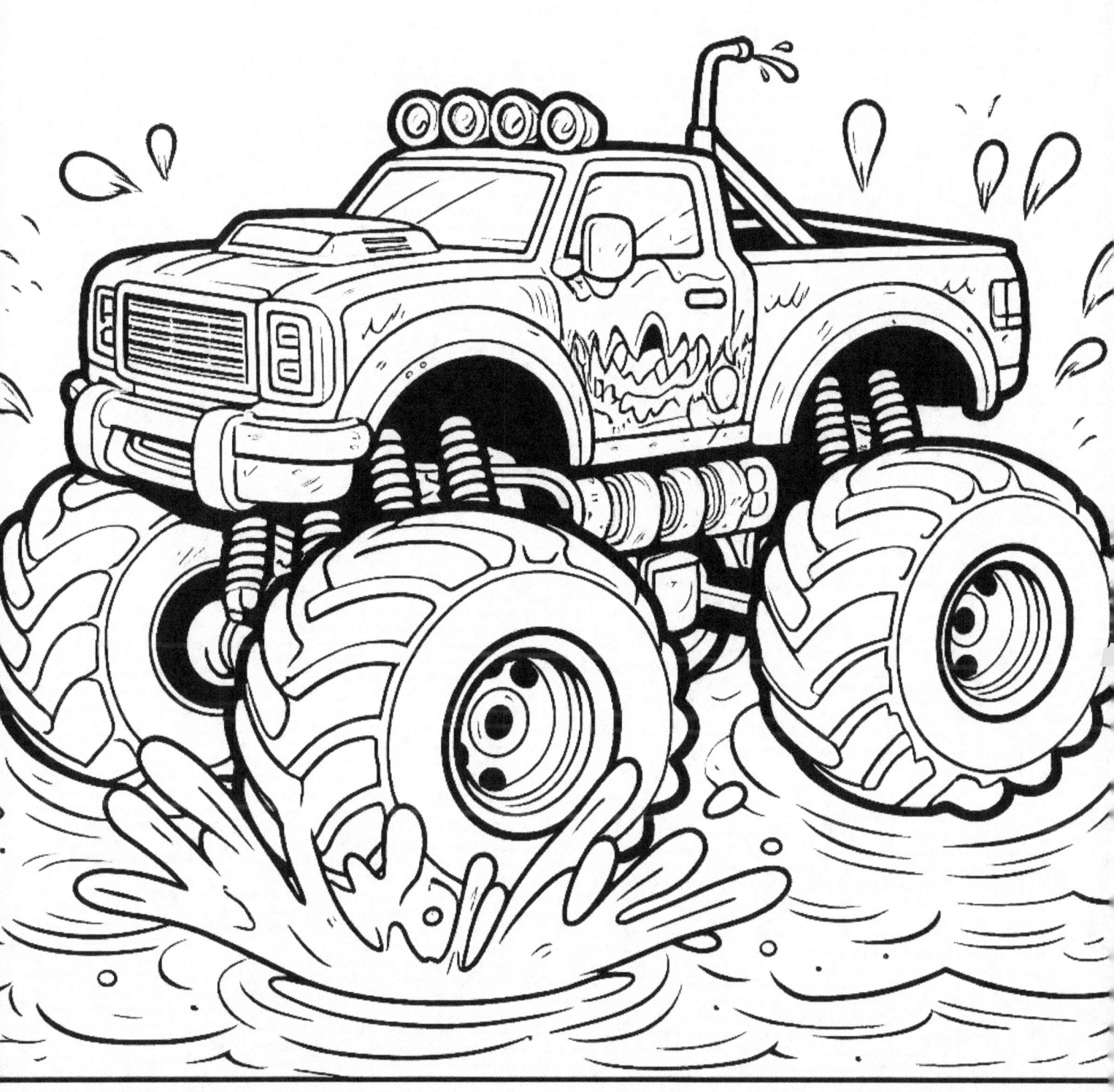

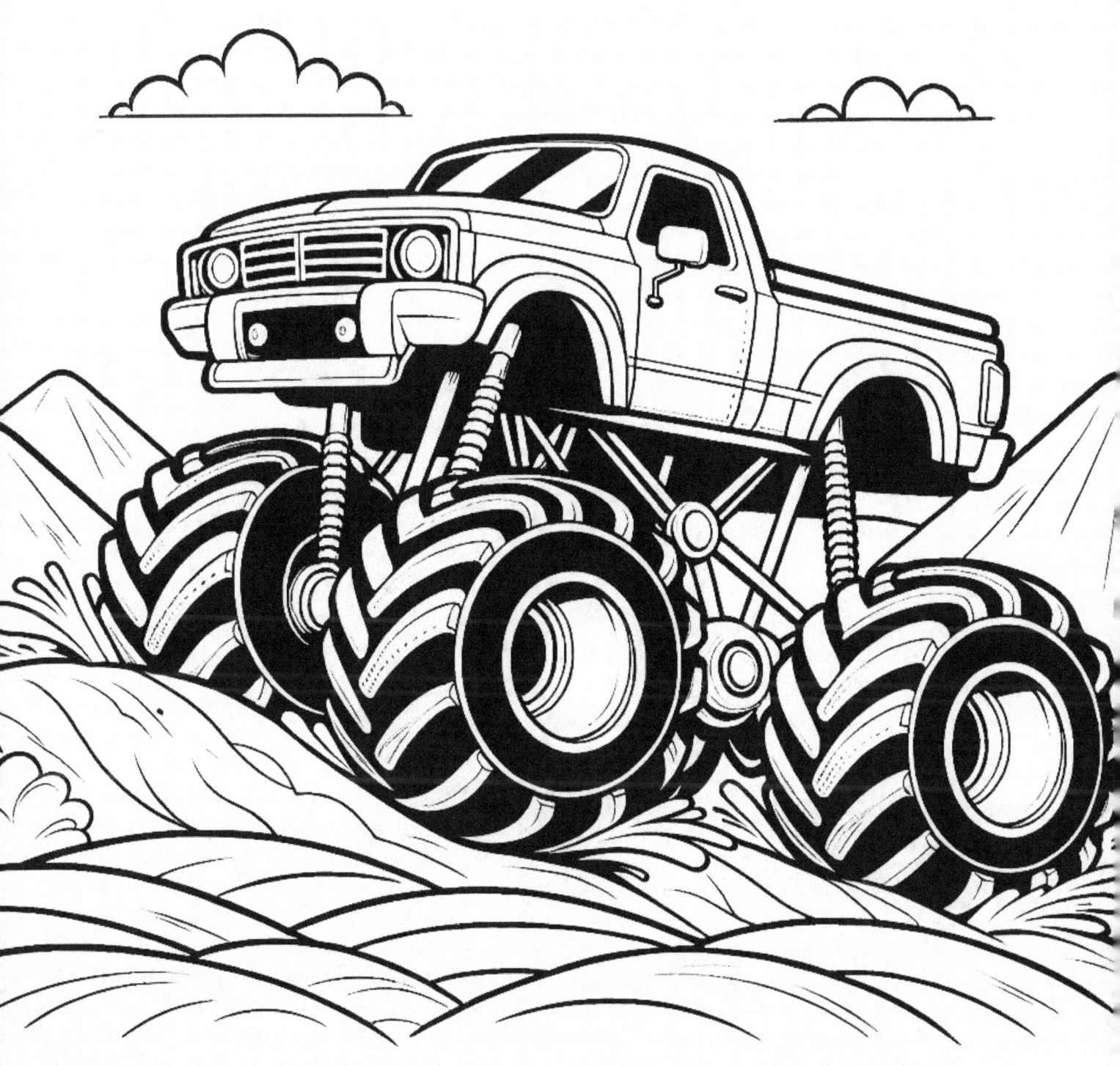

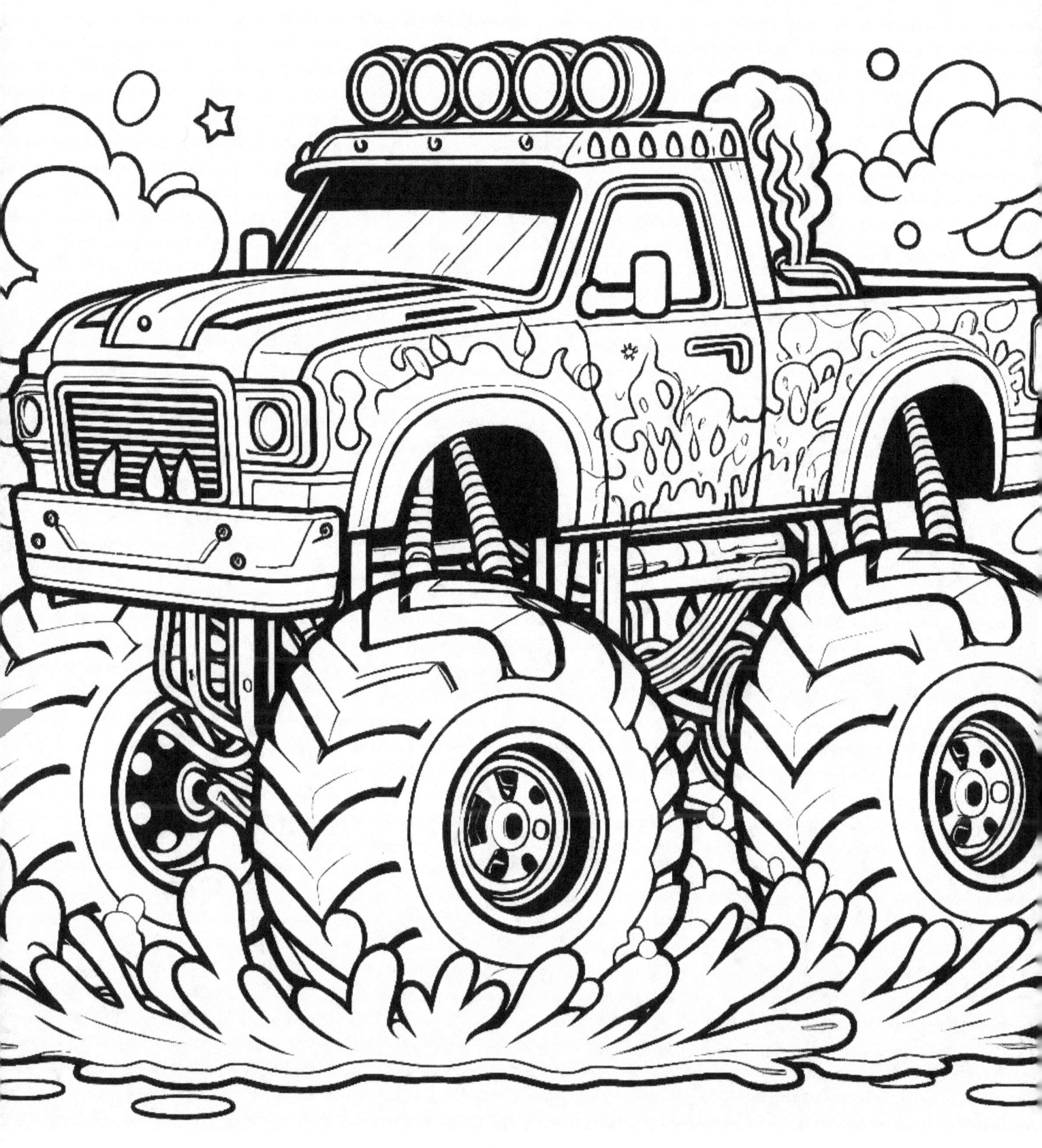

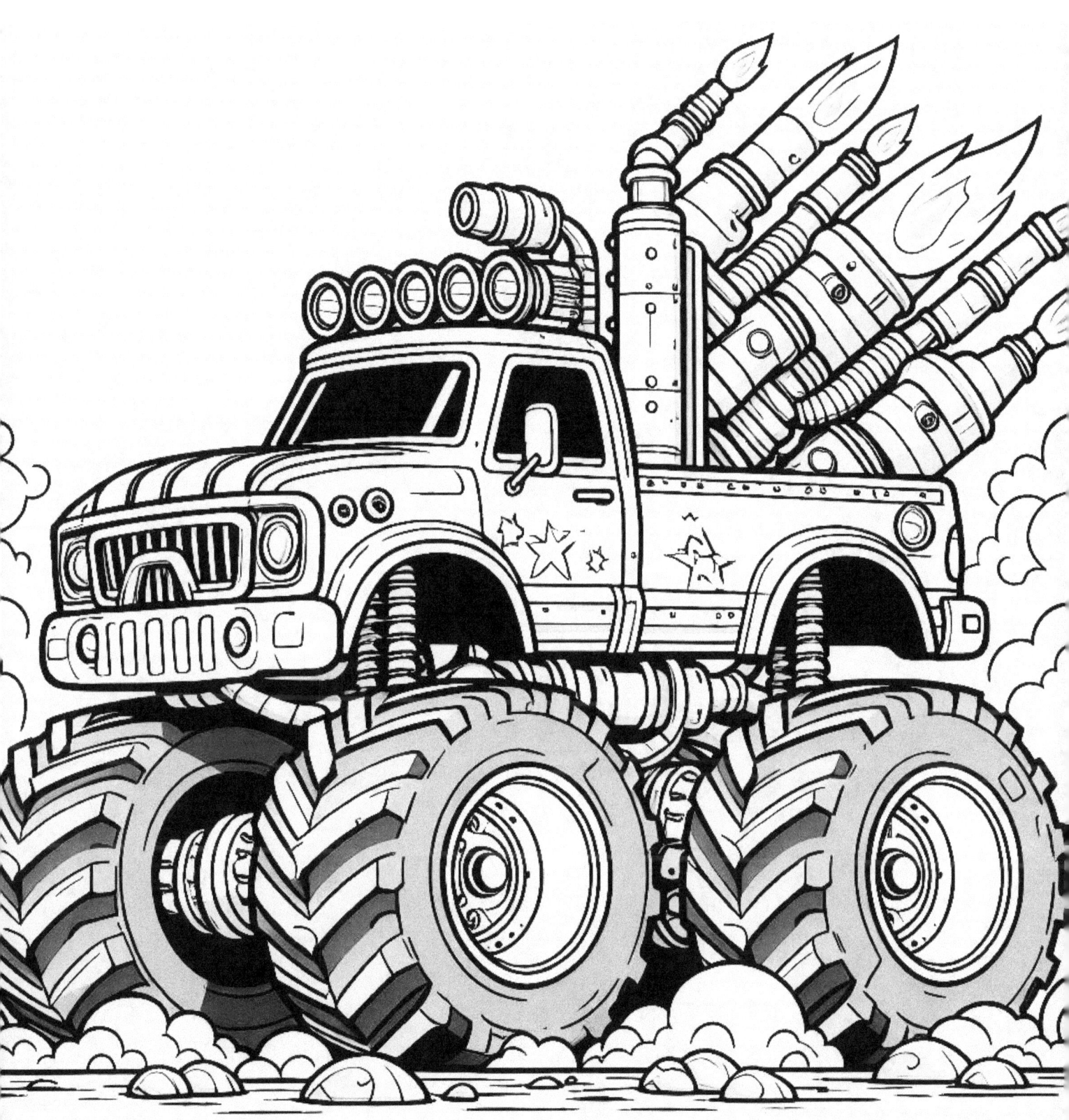

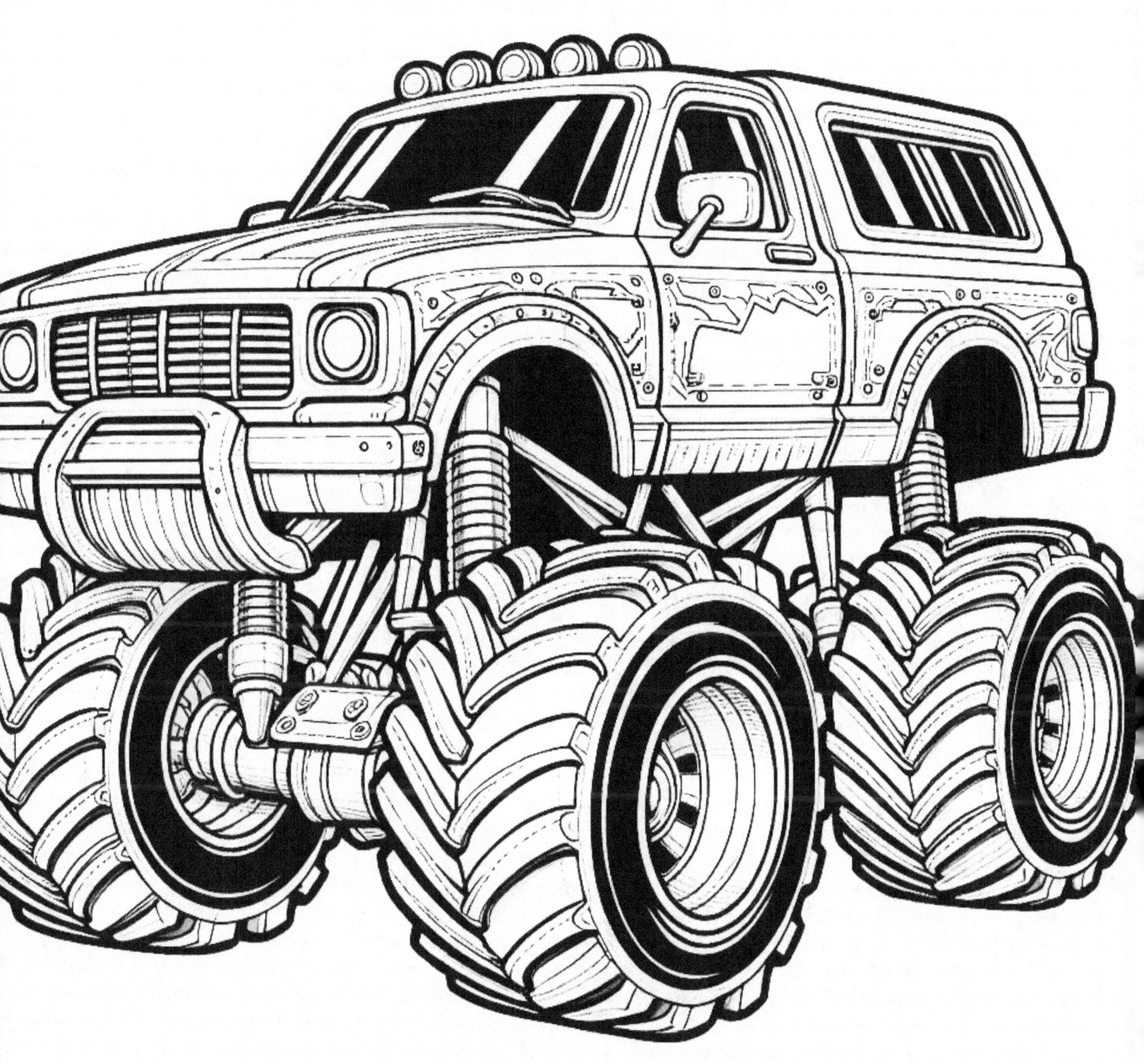

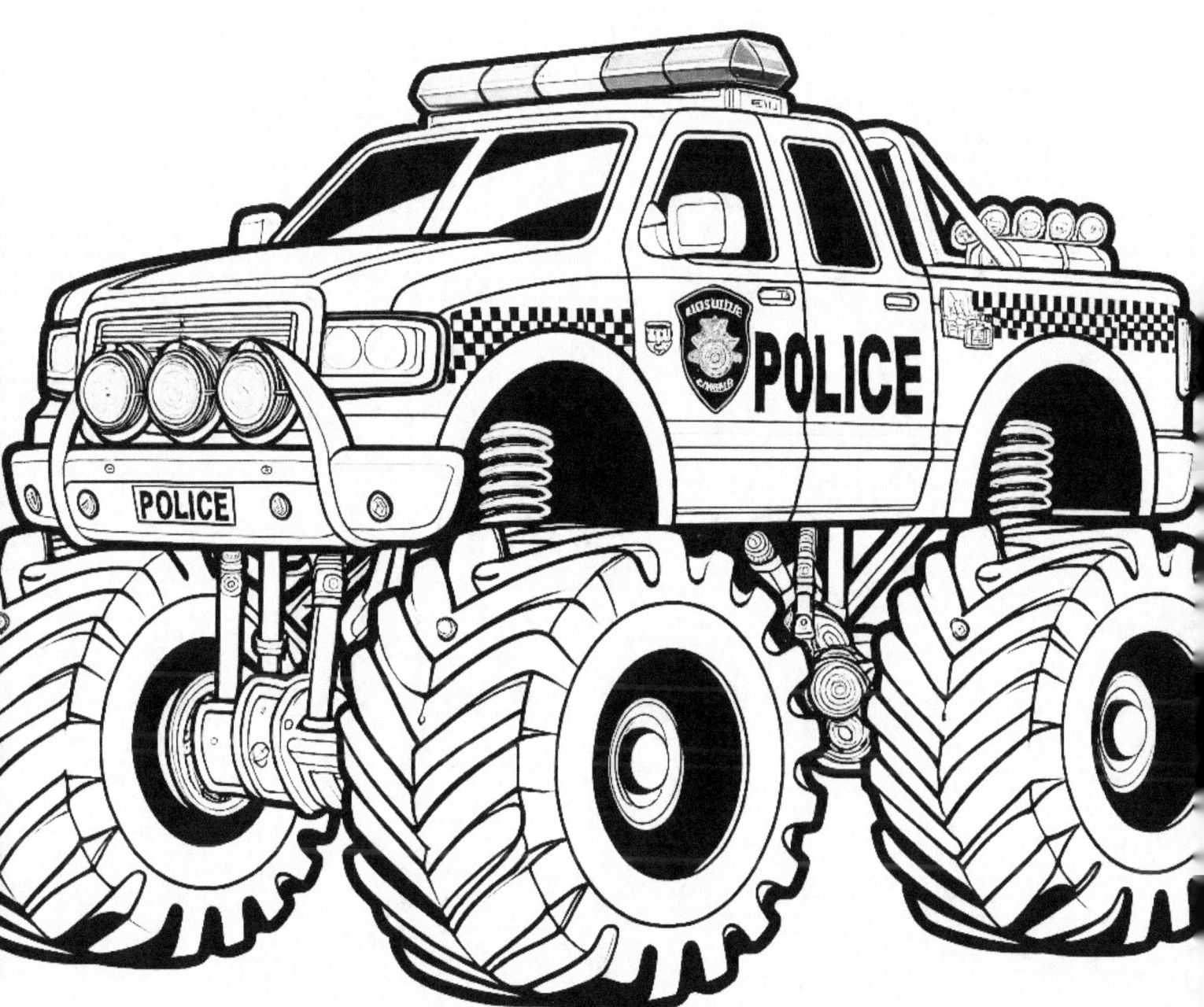

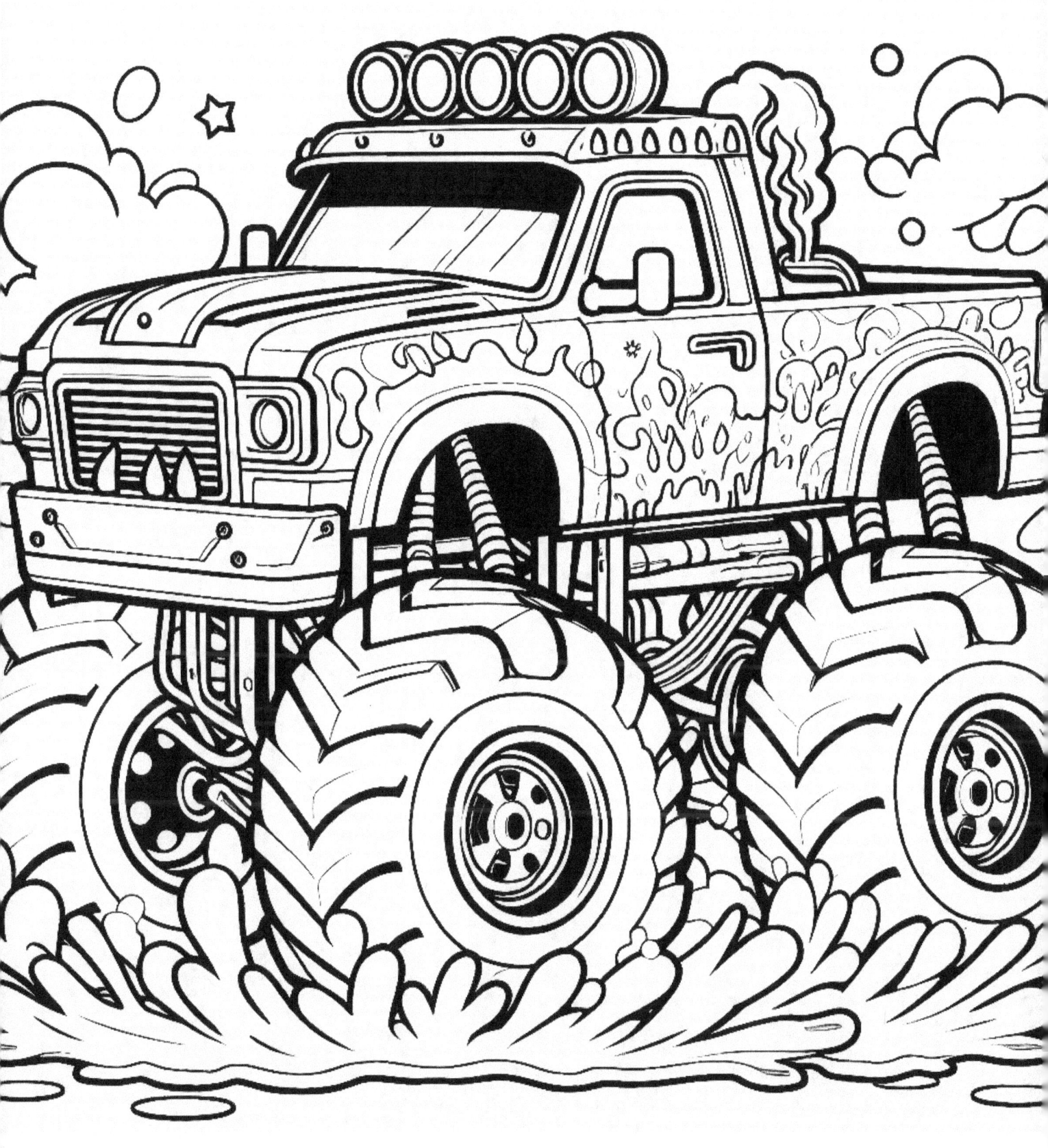

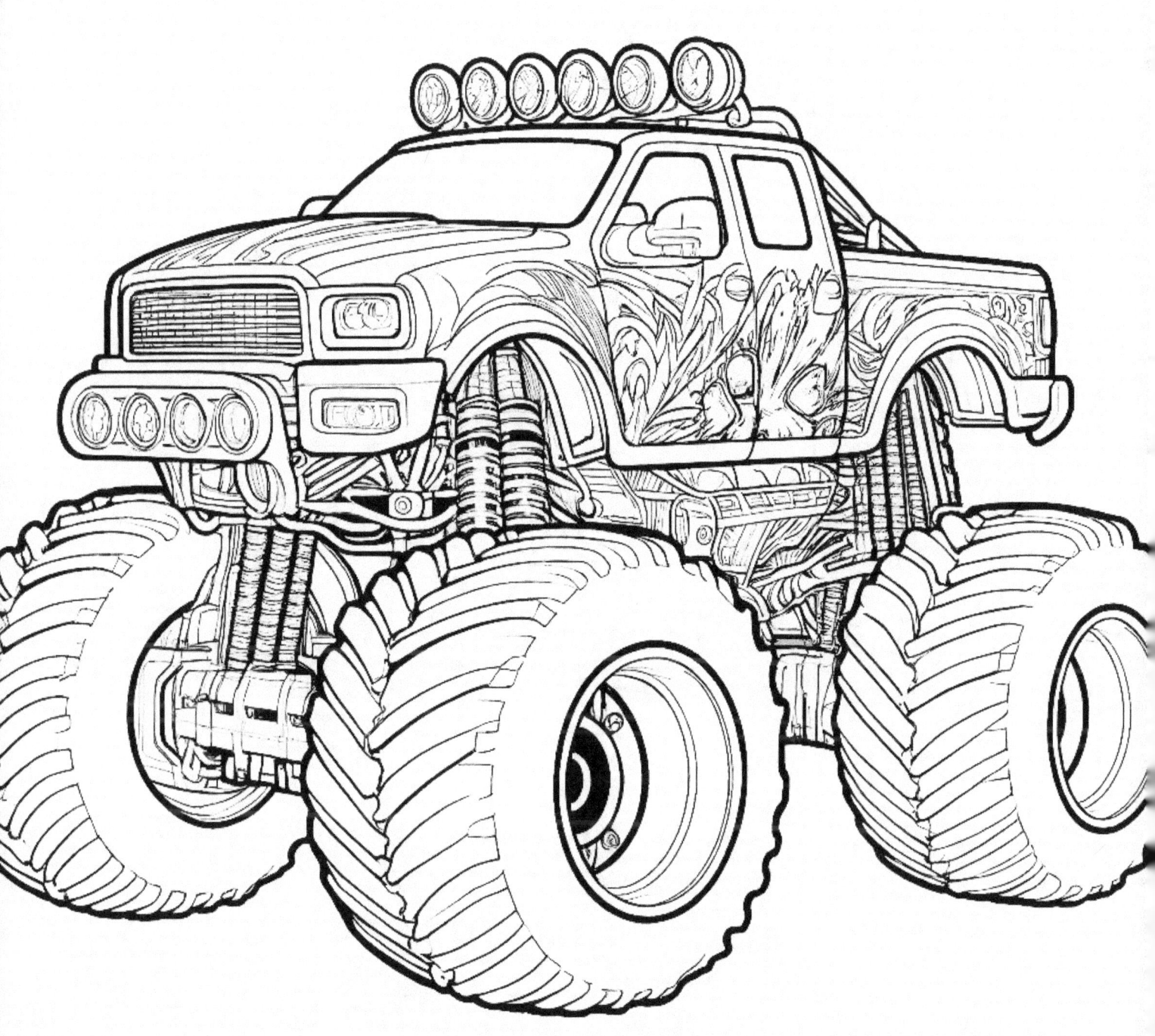

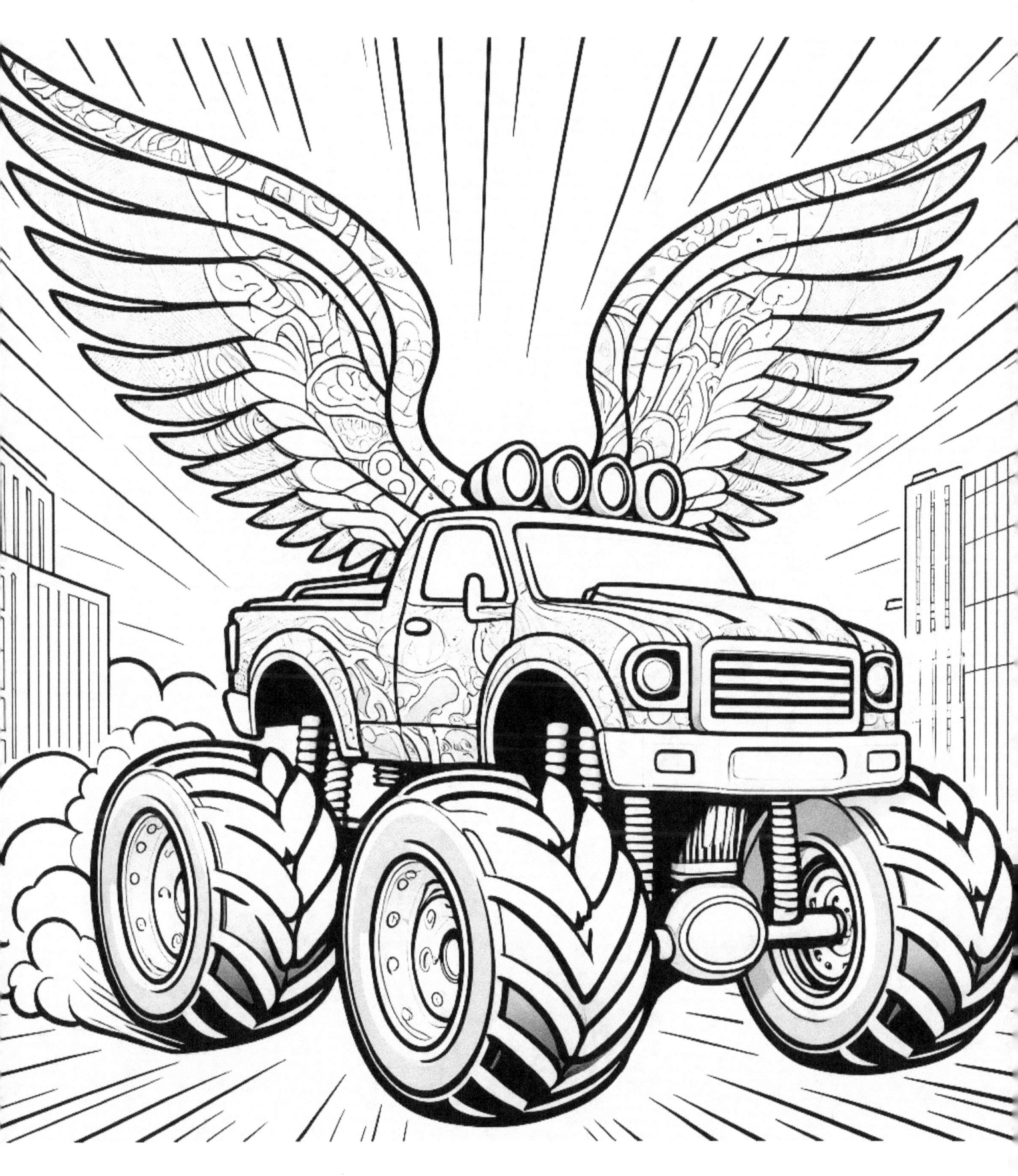

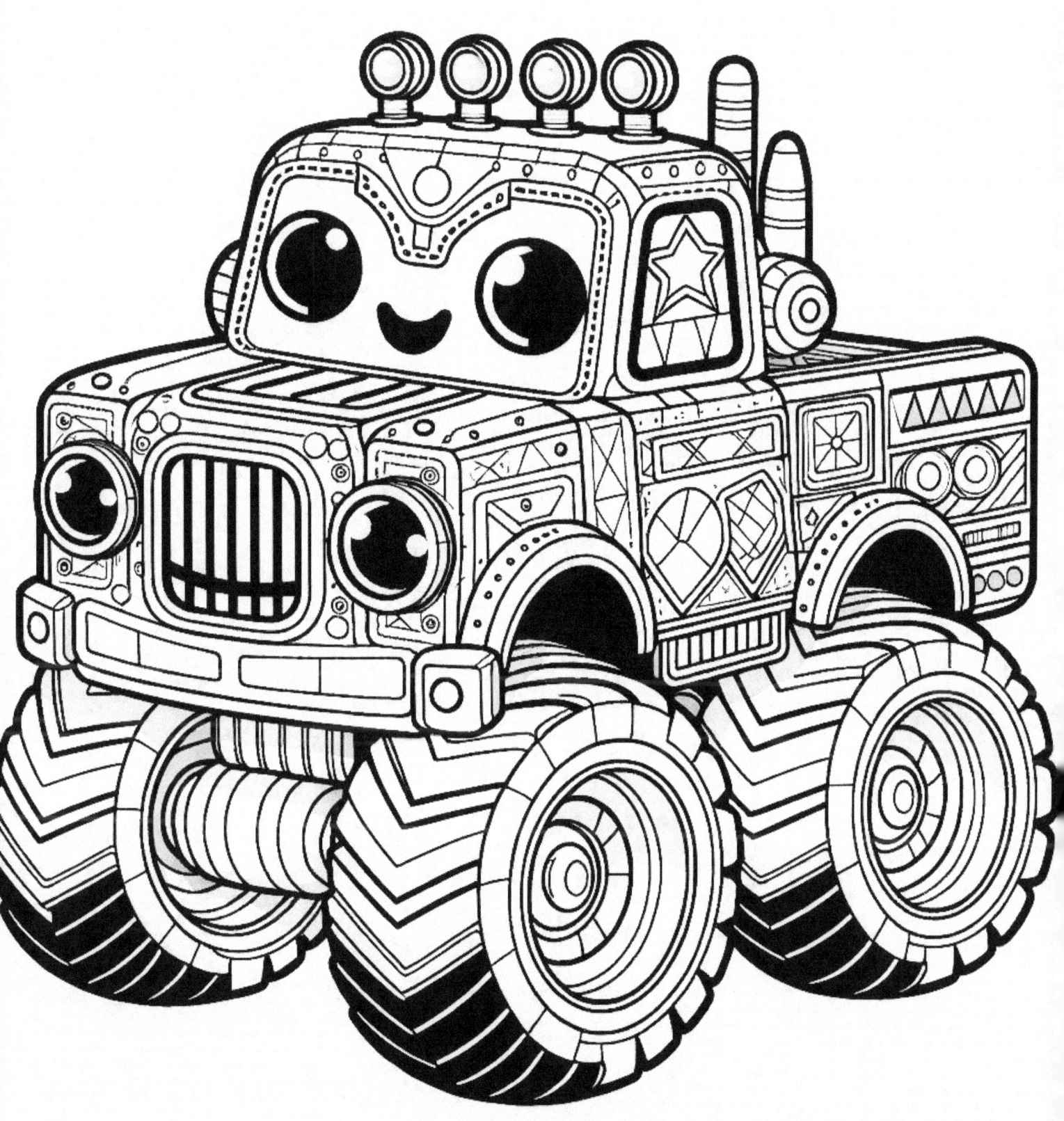

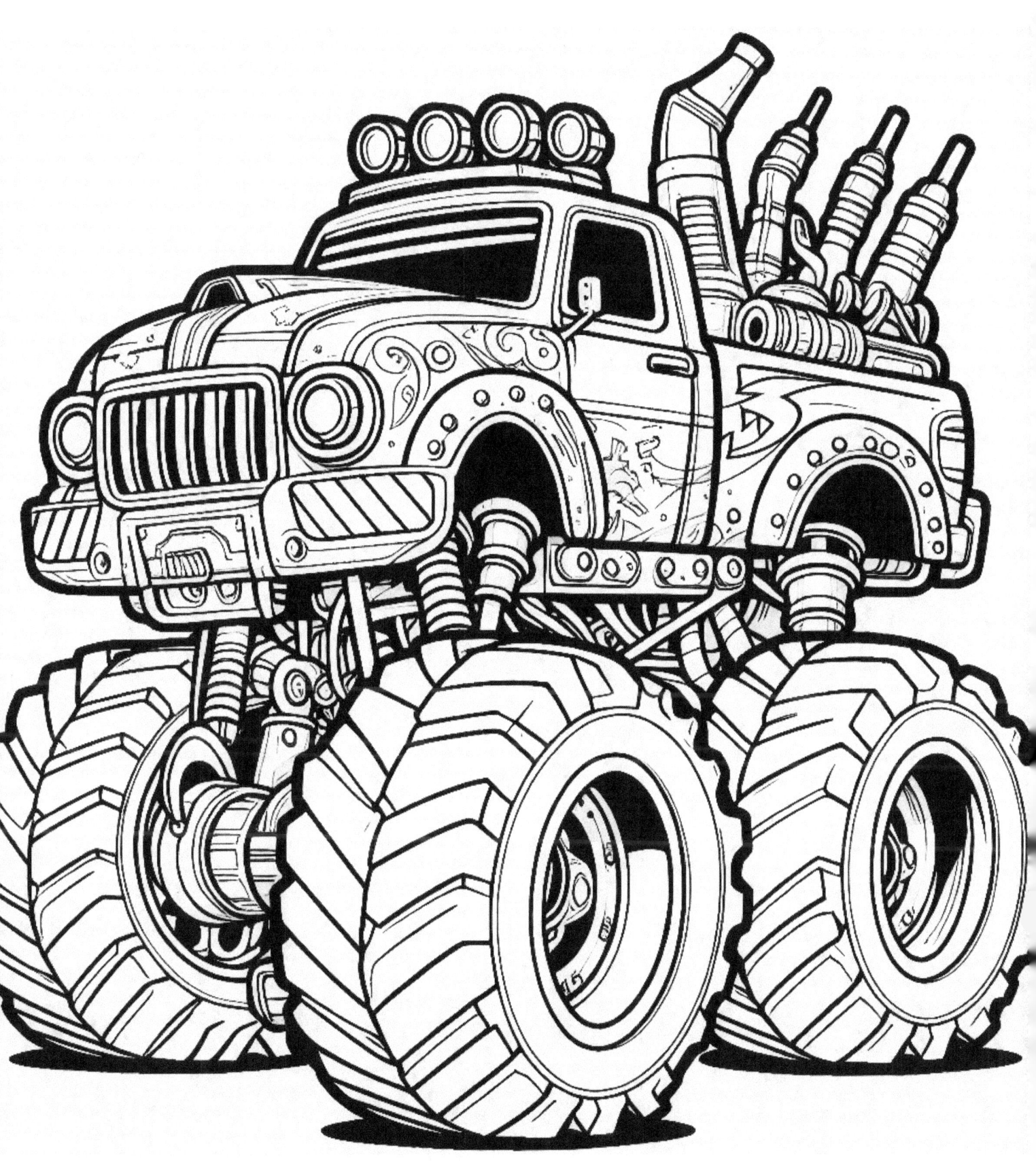

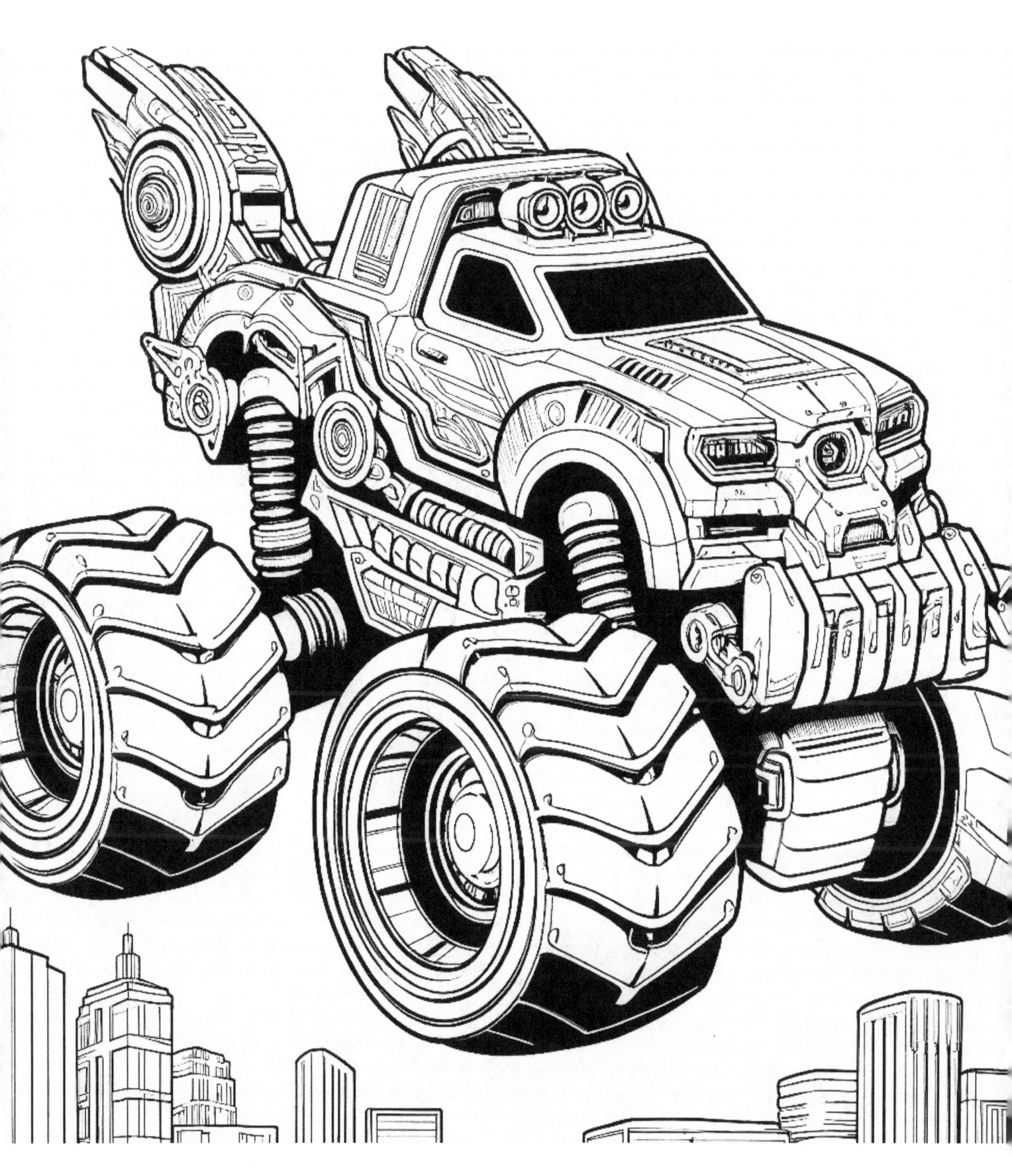

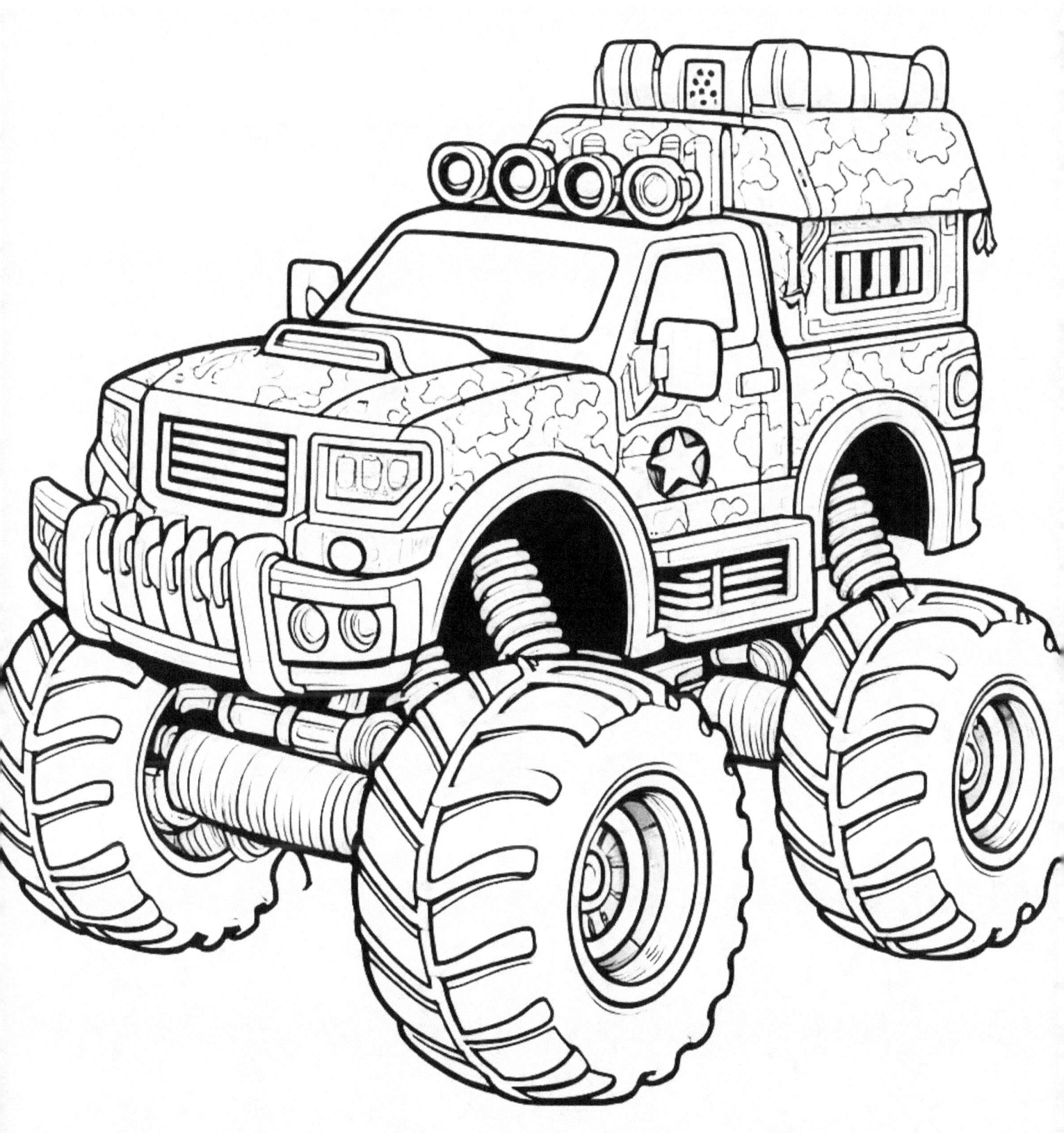

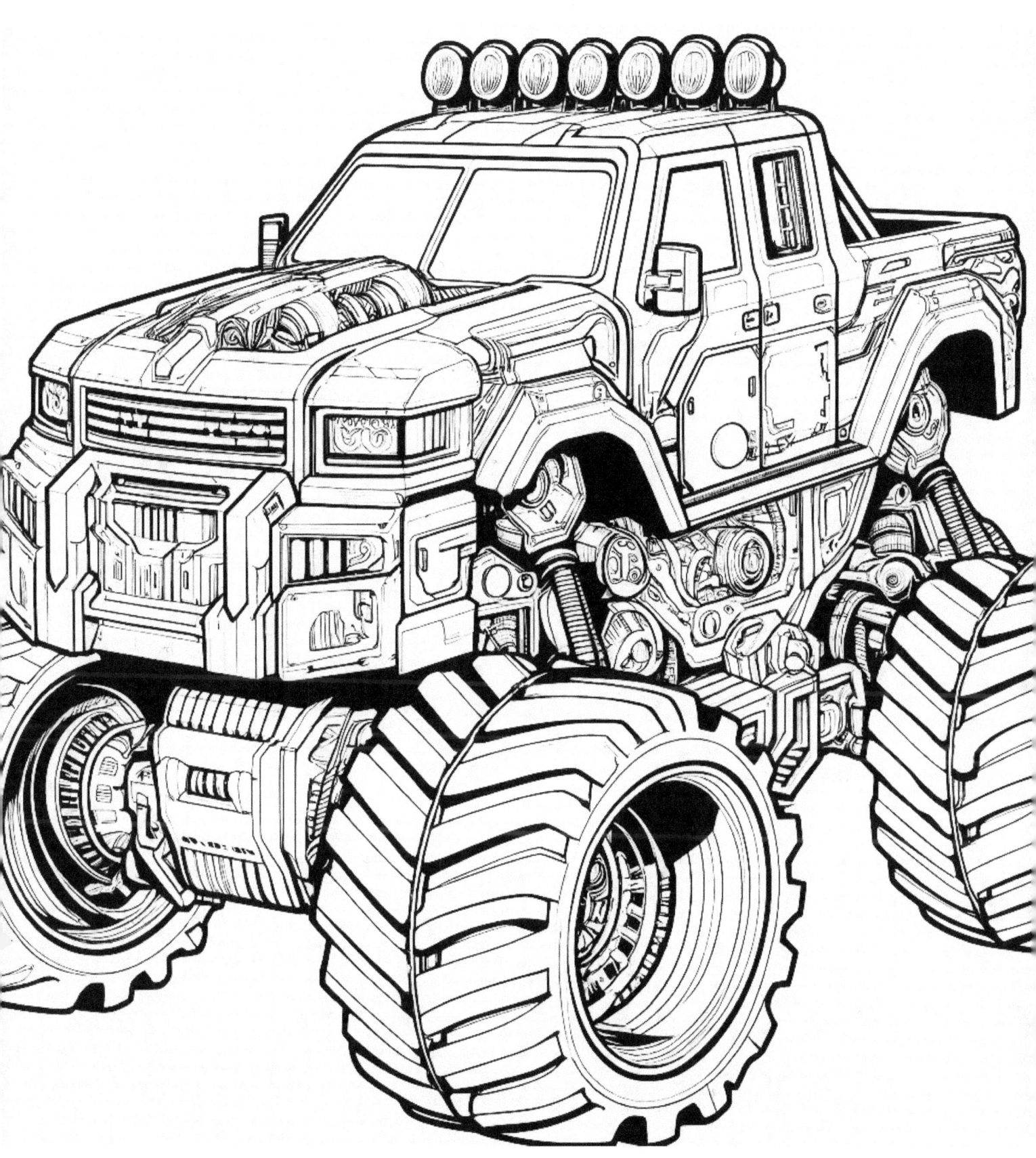

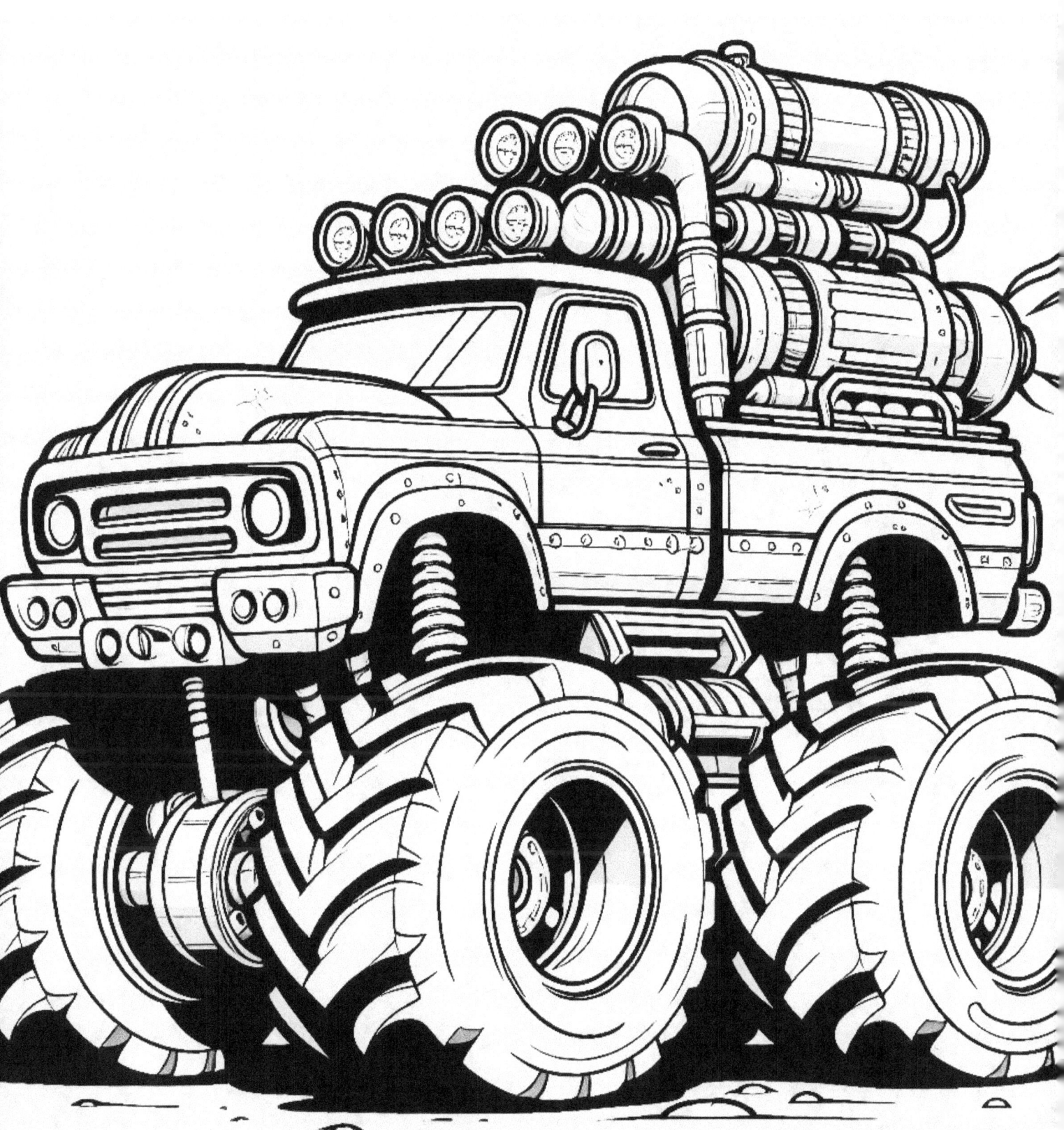

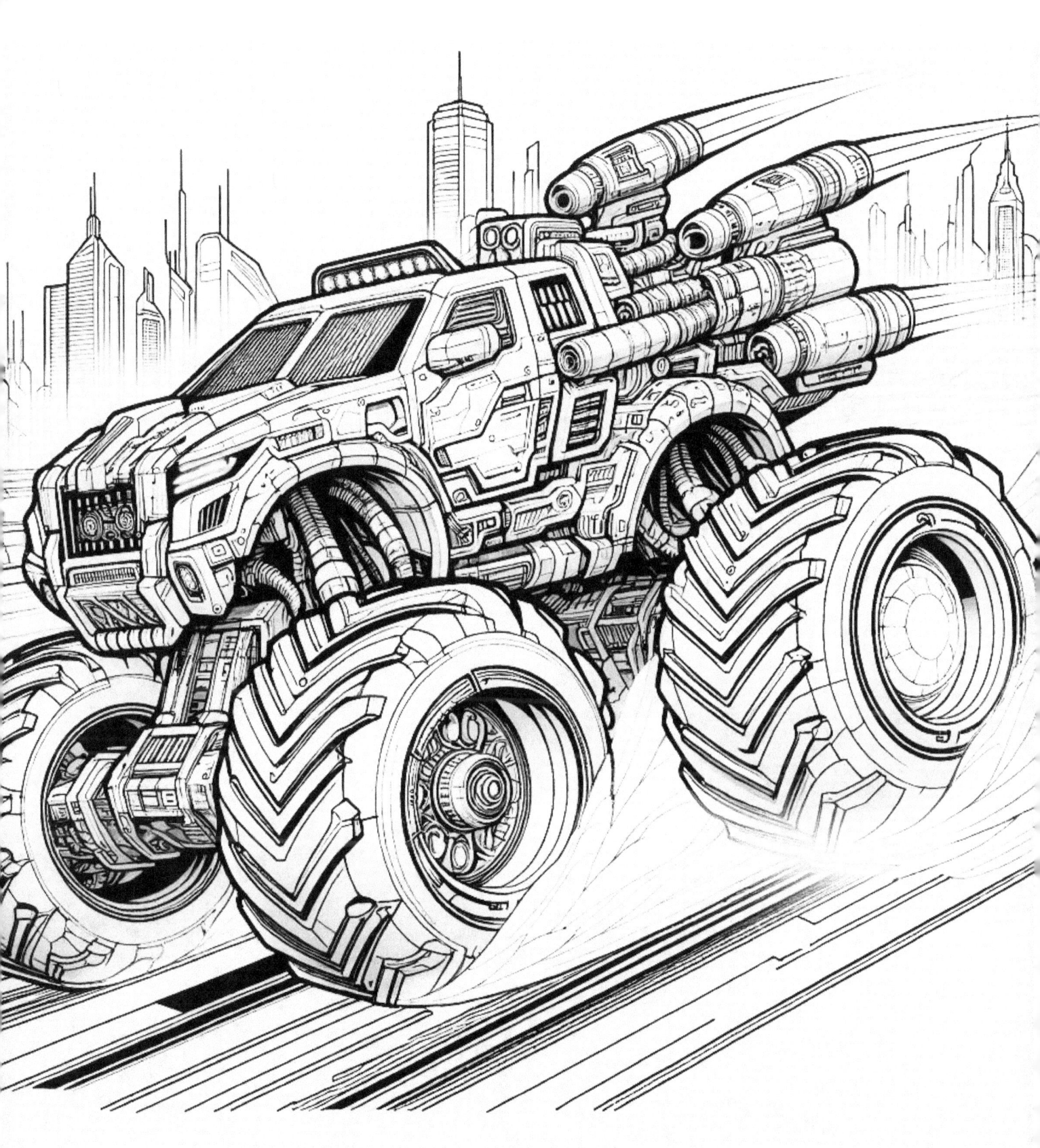

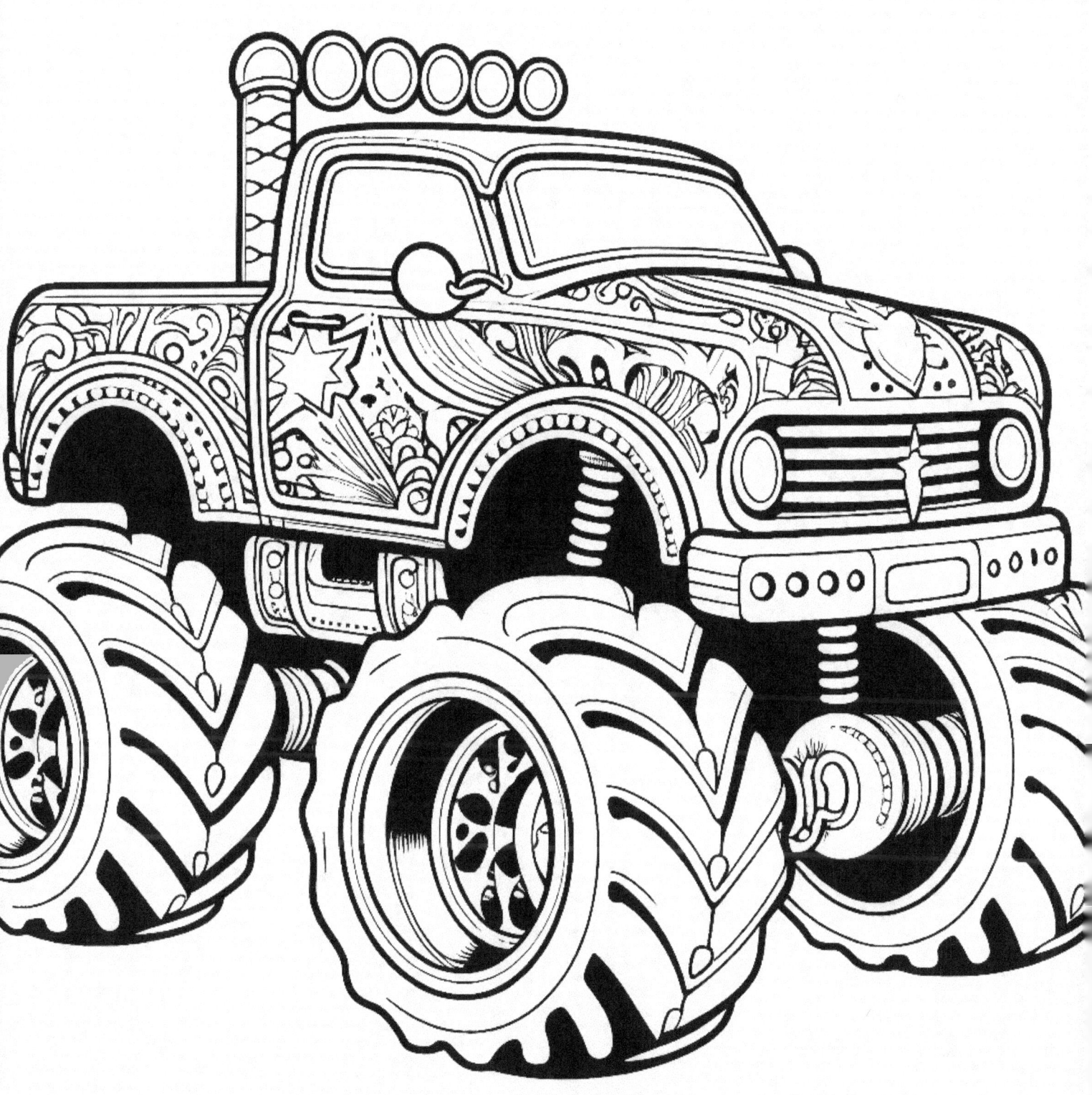

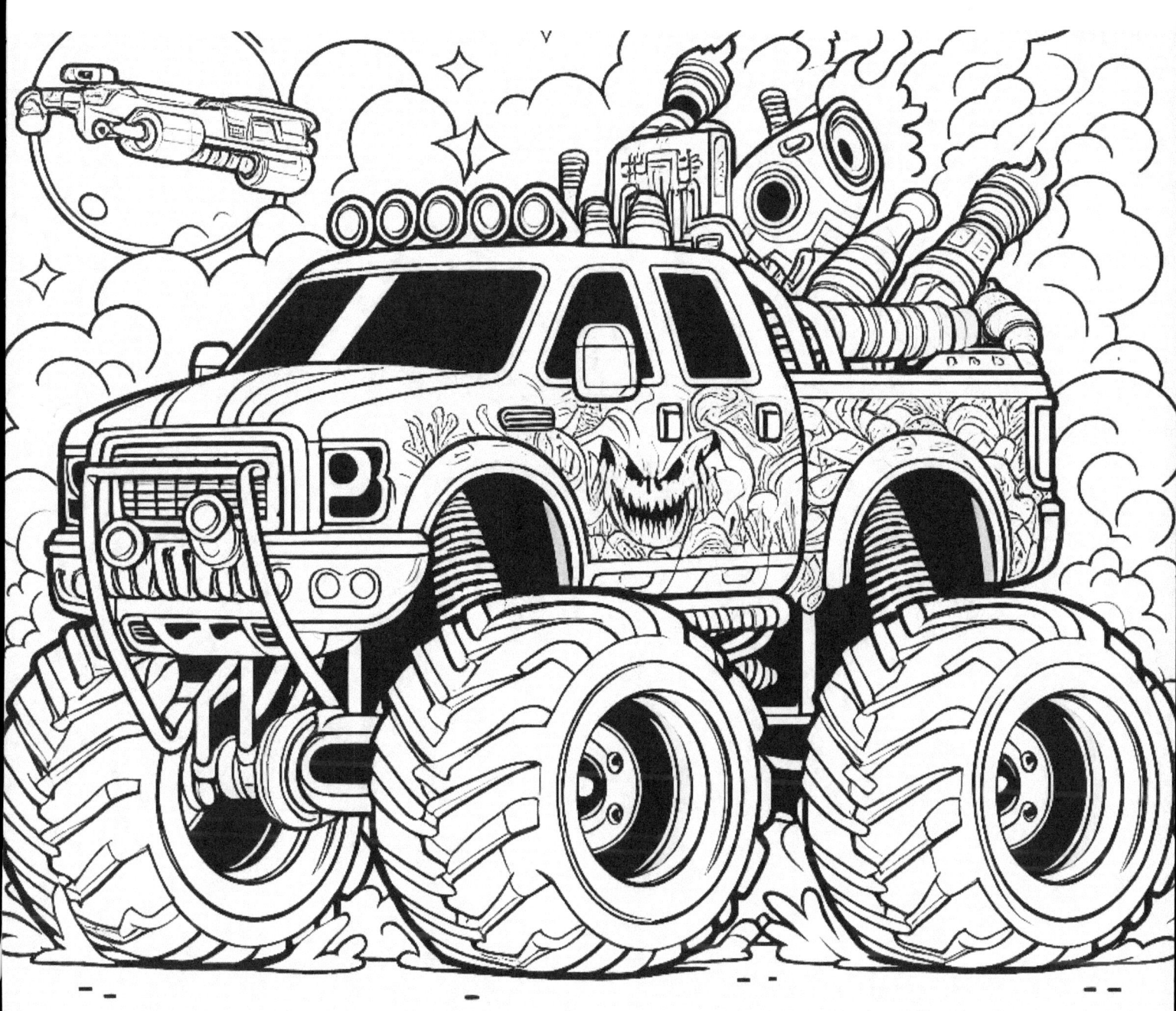